X 7/93
X紅
Sop

000363

Memory

Open Guides to Psychology

Series Editor: Judith Greene, Professor of Psychology at the Open University

Titles in the series

Learning to Use Statistical Tests in Psychology
Judith Greene and Manuela D'Oliveira

Basic Cognitive Processes
Judith Greene and Carolyn Hicks

Memory: A Cognitive Approach
Gillian Cohen, Michael W. Eysenck and Martin E. Le Voi

Language Understanding: A Cognitive Approach
Judith Greene

Problem Solving: A Cognitive Approach
Hank Kahney

Perception and Representation: A Cognitive Approach
Ilona Roth and John Frisby

Titles in preparation

Designing and Reporting Experiments
Peter Harris

Issues in Brain and Behaviour
Frederick Toates

Basic Social Psychology
Dorothy Miell

Memory:
A Cognitive Approach

Gillian Cohen
Michael W. Eysenck
and
Martin E. Le Voi

Open University Press
Milton Keynes · Philadelphia

Open University Press
12 Cofferidge Close
Stony Stratford
Milton Keynes MK11 1BY, England
and
1900 Frost Road, Suite 101
Bristol, PA 19007, USA

First published 1986. Reprinted 1988, 1989

British Library Cataloguing in Publication Data
Cohen, Gillian
    Memory: a cognitive approach. — (Open guides to
    psychology).
    1. Memory
    I. Title   II. Eysenck, Michael W.   III. Le Voi,
    Martin E.   IV. Series
    153.1'2   BF371

    ISBN 0-335-15325-9

Library of Congress Cataloging in Publication Data
Cohen, Gillian
    Memory: a cognitive approach.
    Bibliography: p.
    Includes indexes.
    1. Memory. 2. Cognition. I. Eysenck, Michael W.
    II.   Le Voi, Martin E.   III. Title.
    [DNLM: 1. Memory. BF371 C678m]
    BF371.C58 1986   153.1'2   85-19866

    ISBN 0-335-15325-9 (pbk.)

Phototypeset by Dobbie Typesetting Service, Plymouth, Devon
Printed in Great Britain at the Alden Press, Oxford

Memory: A Cognitive Approach

Contents

Part II   Working Memory
Michael W. Eysenck

Part III   Encoding and Retrieval
in Recognition and Recall
Martin Le Voi

Preface

Within the Open Guides to Psychology series *Memory: A Cognitive Approach* is one of a companion set of four books, the others being *Language Understanding: A Cognitive Approach; Problem Solving: A Cognitive Approach;* and *Perception and Representation: A Cognitive Approach.* Together these form the main texts of the Open University third level course in Cognitive Psychology, but each of the four volumes can be read independently. The course is designed for second or third year students. It is presented in the style and format that the Open University has found to be uniquely effective in making the material intelligible and interesting.

The books provide an up-to-date in-depth treatment of the major issues, theories and findings in cognitive psychology. They are designed to introduce a representative selection of different research methods, and the reader is encouraged, by means of Activities and Self-assessment Questions interpolated through the text, to become involved in cognitive psychology as an active participant.

The authors gratefully acknowledge the many helpful comments and suggestions of fellow members of the course team on earlier drafts, and the valuable assistance of Doreen Warwick in typing the manuscript.

Acknowledgements

Grateful acknowledgement is made to the following for material used in this book:

Figure 1.1 from L. R. Peterson and M. J. Peterson, 'Short term retention of individual items', in *Journal of Experimental Psychology*, vol. 58, 1959;

Figure 2.6 from G. J. Hitch and A. D. Baddeley, 'Verbal reasoning and working memory', in *Quarterly Journal of Experimental Psychology*, vol. 28, 1976, Academic Press.

Introduction

This book is divided into three parts each dealing with a different aspect of memory. Part I is about Everyday Memory and is concerned with the way memory functions in everyday life. The reader will be on familiar ground here because everybody has first-hand experience on the way his or her own memory works in similar circumstances. The research discussed in this part focuses primarily on the contents of everyday memory, on what we remember and what we forget. While some things are remembered accurately, a great deal of what we experience in daily life is forgotten or misremembered. Several theories that have been proposed to explain the selective nature of everyday memory are outlined and discussed.

Parts II and III are concerned with the processes and mechanisms of memory. Part II deals with Working Memory and is concerned with the processing activities that occur when memories are input to the system. Part III is about Encoding and Retrieval of memories and deals with the way memories are stored and the way they are retrieved. So, roughly speaking, these two parts respectively address the problems of how information gets into the memory system and how it gets out again. The theoretical construct of Working Memory corresponds to short-term memory but emphasizes the idea that information in Working Memory may be manipulated, transformed or utilized in ongoing cognitive tasks like talking and reading, doing mental arithmetic or reasoning. Working Memory is not just a receptacle in which information is temporarily dumped. The retrieval processes described in Part III are directed toward the retrieval of information from memory. One of the more frustrating characteristics of human memory is the way that putting an item of information into store is no guarantee that it can be retrieved again later on demand. This part discusses various theoretical explanations for the success or failure of the retrieval process. In the final Overview an attempt is made to show briefly how the different approaches to memory discussed separately in each part are inter-related.

This book does not cover every aspect of human memory. Because all higher mental processes rely on memory, memory is involved in every area of cognitive psychology. In consequence, all the Cognitive Psychology volumes in the Open Guides to Psychology series cannot help but discuss the role of memory. One important issue in the study of memory concerns the way information is represented. Just as a given piece of information might be represented externally in sentences, in

a table of numbers, in a graph, a picture or a diagram, so there are
a variety of different forms that an internalized mental representation
might take. Different kinds of memory representations underlie
different cognitive activities, such as perception, language, and problem
solving; these aspects of the memory system are considered separately
in the three companion volumes to this Open Guide.

How to use this guide

In each part of this book the reader will find Activities and Self-
Assessment Questions (SAQs) inserted at various points in the text.
Doing the Activities will give a deeper insight and a better
understanding of how some of the research techniques work. It is
particularly important to carry out the Activities in Part III carefully
and to understand the scoring system used in the first of these activities,
since the techniques that are demonstrated form the basis of much
of the discussion that follows. The SAQs provide the reader with a
means of checking his or her understanding. The answers can be found
at the end of the book and will help to illuminate points made in the
text.

Doing the Activities and answering the SAQs engages the reader
as an active participant instead of just a passive recipient. He or she
is forced to carry out the kind of deeper level processing described
in Part II which is known to produce better comprehension and
retention of what is read.

Detailed accounts of experiments are presented in Techniques Boxes
and these are chosen as illustrative of representative experimental
methods. The Summaries recapitulate the main points in each section
and provide a useful aid to revision. The Index of Concepts that
appears at the end of the book allows the reader to locate the place
in the text where a concept is first introduced and defined. Entries
in the Index of Concepts are italicized in the text.

Each part concludes with a short list of recommended further
reading. Obviously the interested reader can also follow up the
references given in the text. Some of these references are to articles
in *Issues in Cognitive Modeling*, edited by Aitkenhead and Slack, which
is the Reader for the Open University course in Cognitive Psychology.
This is designed to be a companion volume to the other Cognitive
Psychology volumes in the Open Guides to Psychology series.

Part I
Everyday Memory

Gillian Cohen

Contents

1   Introduction:
The hundred years of silence

Psychologists have been studying memory for a hundred years. What is there to show for it? Many fascinating questions are thrown up by our day-to-day experience of the way our memories seem to work, and you might think that all these puzzles would have been solved long ago. Do old people really remember the distant past better than the recent past? Why do people who share exactly the same experience remember it differently? Why are certain episodes in our lives remembered in vivid detail when so much else seems to be lost without a trace? Why do we remember so little from the first years of our lives?

In 1978 Ulric Neisser drew attention to the 'thundering silence' with which psychologists responded when confronted with questions like these. The past hundred years had been spent in the laboratory concentrating almost entirely on theoretical questions about the underlying mechanisms of memory. Ordinary practical questions about how memory functions in daily life in the real world had not been considered important. One of the few exceptions is the work of Bartlett (1932). He did study memory for realistic material like stories, faces and pictures, but his ideas did not have much influence at that time.

Although laboratory experiments do not always shed light on remembering and forgetting in the world outside, working in laboratory conditions has many obvious advantages. It allows the experimenter to control rigorously the nature of the to-be-remembered material, the duration and timing of the presentation, the test environment, the instructions to the subject, the conditions under which the task is carried out, and so on. Techniques Box A shows a typical experiment of this kind, in which these factors are carefully regulated and standardized.

TECHNIQUES BOX A

Peterson and Peterson's Trigram Retention Experiment (1959)

Rationale
Peterson and Peterson wanted to study the rate of 'pure' short-term forgetting when no rehearsal is allowed.

Method
Their stimuli consisted of three consonants (called a trigram), which had to be recalled after an interval of 3–18 seconds during which time subjects did an interpolated task to prevent them rehearsing. The experiment consisted of many trials, each consisting of the following sequence:

15

1   A trigram (e.g. XPJ) was presented acoustically (i.e. read out aloud).
2   A three-digit number was presented acoustically (e.g. 'four hundred and thirty six').
3   Subjects counted backwards aloud in threes (e.g. 436, 433, 430, 427, 424, etc.). This is the interpolated task.
4   Subjects continued to count for either 3, 6, 9, 12, 15, or 18 seconds, at the end of which time a tone signal was heard.
5   At the tone signal, subjects stopped counting backwards, and attempted to recall the trigram.

Results

Peterson and Peterson scored the subjects' recall, marking letters correct only when they were reported in the same place in the sequence as in the original. For example, if a subject recalled 'XJP' for 'XPJ', he or she was scored as recalling only one correct item. The results are shown in Figure 1.1. The average percentage correct recall of trigrams is high with short delays, but falls as the delay period increases. After 18 seconds of delay, subjects were correctly recalling only just over 10 per cent of the trigrams.

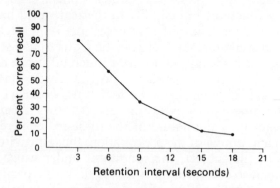

Figure 1.1   The percentage of trigrams correctly recalled, as a function of delay before recall (Peterson and Peterson, 1959)

The fact that material in short-term memory (STM) is forgotten within a period of 6–12 seconds if it is not rehearsed was interpreted by Peterson and Peterson as evidence of the rate of decay of a short-term memory trace.

The results of laboratory experiments like this one are important for constructing and testing theoretical models of memory and for establishing parameters of the memory mechanism such as the rate of decay for items in short-term memory. Even so, studying memory in the laboratory is very different from studying memory in real life.

Think about the kind of things you have to remember on a typical day. These might include a shopping list, a recipe, telephoning a relative, filling the car up with petrol, the arguments put forward at a meeting and the plot of a television play. The things we have to remember in the world outside the laboratory are not isolated lists of meaningless items. They include complex experiences in the past, plans for the future, facts and scenes embedded in a rich context of ongoing events and surrounding objects. When we encounter the stuff of real-life memories we are often inattentive, distracted or confused. Such memories may be recalled repeatedly, or may lie dormant for many years. Because the workings of everyday memory are so complicated and confused, there are many factors that cannot be measured or controlled and observations are often imprecise. Ideally, the two approaches should be complementary. We need the theoretical framework derived from more rigorous experimental studies in order to interpret everyday memory phenomena, and to try to draw some general conclusions about them. And, if theorizing is not to be sterile, it needs to be applied to the world outside the laboratory.

Since 1978 the hundred years of silence have come to an end. Psychology has responded to Neisser's challenge and work on everyday memory is booming. This new wave of interest in the practical applied aspects of cognitive psychology is not confined to the study of memory. Vigorous efforts are under way to relate many areas of psychology to the mental activities of ordinary people going about their daily lives. Problems such as how doctors decide on a medical diagnosis, the reliability of witnesses in courts, the perceptual processes that underlie face recognition, and the skills involved in holding conversations, scheduling jobs to be done and planning routes, are all being studied. This kind of research has what Neisser termed *ecological validity*. This means that it is based on real situations in real environments, and the findings arising from it have real applications. Neisser has been a strong advocate of ecological validity, and many psychologists engaged in the study of thinking have followed his lead.

1.1   *Methods for studying everyday memory*

Researchers engaged in the realistic study of memory cannot just go about making observations of naturally occurring memory activities. To be informative, any research, even naturalistic research, must be guided by specific questions. The researcher must narrow the scope of inquiry so as to focus on some particular aspects of memory, and must devise some methods of testing or measuring how well memory works.

Two main approaches have been adopted. The first relies on *self-reports* or introspections, recording people's own observations about the way their memories function, about the things they remember and the things they forget. The second approach retains the methods of formal experimentation, but attempts to devise *naturalistic experiments* which are much more representative of real life. This usually involves asking people to remember natural material such as stories, films, or maps, instead of the traditional lists of letters, words or digits. In Part I of this volume we shall examine some examples of both kinds of research into everyday memory.

The use of self-reports by present-day psychologists is something of a turn around. Early psychologists like Wundt and Freud relied heavily on introspections as evidence for their theories, but self-reports were discredited during the Behaviourist era (roughly from the 1920s to the 1950s), when interest was focused on overt behaviour and the importance, and even existence, of mental events were discounted. Now psychologists who study thinking have begun to turn back the clock and the old introspective methods have been cautiously resurrected and brought back into use.

It is recognized that many of the very rapid mental processes that underlie activities like perceiving a complex scene, recognizing a word, or speaking a grammatical sentence, are simply not accessible to consciousness. In these cases, we are aware of the end product of the mental operations, but not of the processes themselves. People cannot introspect and make verbal reports about what is going on in their heads below the level of consciousness and we must accept that a lot of mental activity is unconscious. Nevertheless, there are some thought processes that do take place consciously and with some effort and practice people can become quite good at describing them. This is particularly true of so-called 'slow processes' — long drawn out mental processes like the strategies involved in solving problems, or attempts to reconstruct a memory from the past.

No method of psychological investigation is entirely foolproof and watertight. Self-reports may be unreliable if people exaggerate or distort them. People may not like to reveal the confused and muddled state of their mental processes, and may tidy up the reported version so as to seem more impressive. It is up to the researcher to guard against this and persuade subjects to be as accurate as possible. A more detailed discussion of the validity of introspective reports as evidence of mental processes is given in the article by George Miller in Aitkenhead and Slack (1985).

Which of the following mental operations do you think would be 'accessible to introspection' so that someone could describe the mental processes involved? Which would be inaccessible to introspection? Why?
(a) Dividing 246 by 3.
(b) Considering a move at chess or draughts.
(c) Writing your own name.
(d) Recognizing a tune.
(e) Solving a crossword puzzle clue.

Naturalistic experiments also have some pitfalls. An experimental situation is never exactly representative of real life. Experimental subjects may be anxious about their performance when they know they will be tested; the task may seem pointless or boring, and the material, however realistic, is likely to be more simplified and orderly than real events. Psychologists who opt to study everyday memory have to accept these limitations, but are compensated by the relevance and interest of their findings.

Summary of Section 1

● Traditional laboratory experiments on memory are theoretically important but are too artificial to tell us much about memory in everyday life. These experiments are concerned with the *mechanisms* of memory rather than the *contents* of memory.
● A new wave of interest in everyday memory has sparked off studies which examine the working of memory in real-life situations. These are primarily concerned with memory contents — with what is remembered and what is forgotten.
● The methods used to study everyday memory include asking people to describe the working of their own memories (introspective self reports); and designing naturalistic experiments which try to mimic real-life situations as far as possible.

2 Metamemory

Metamemory means knowing what you know, knowing how your memory works, and being able to assess your own memory.

2.1 Self-rating questionnaires

One way in which self-report methods have been employed is by using questionnaires to find out about the kinds of memory abilities used in everyday life. Typically these questionnaires ask people how well they remember various kinds of things, or how often they forget others. Here are some examples of the kinds of questions that are asked. The respondent is asked to rate the frequency of forgetting and to circle the appropriate value. These values are known as *self ratings*.

	Very often	Quite often	Occasionally	Very rarely	Never
How often do you forget appointments?	4	3	2	1	0
How often do you want to tell a joke but find you cannot remember it?	4	3	2	1	0
How often do you forget people's names?	4	3	2	1	0
When you go shopping, how often do you forget items you intended to buy?	4	3	2	1	0
How often do you forget the route to a particular place?	4	3	2	1	0

It is important to be quite clear about what this sort of questionnaire is actually measuring. The rating values obtained do not necessarily reflect memory ability; they reflect *beliefs about* memory ability. If the respondents are honest and accurate these beliefs may correspond with actual memory ability. But can people assess their own memory efficiency accurately? They may be overboastful or overmodest. Even more worryingly, they may fail to remember how often they forget.

Some researchers consider that self ratings obtained from these questionnaires are invalid (i.e. not a true measure of ability) because they do not correlate highly with scores obtained on objective tests of memory ability. Someone who gives good self ratings on the questionnaire may have poor scores in an experimental test like recalling lists of words. But self-assessment methods are not necessarily discredited by this. The questionnaire and the experimental test are measuring different things, and there is really no reason why a person's score in a word list learning experiment should be considered a more valid reflection of his or her memory ability than the same person's own self ratings. Of course, test scores are more rigorous and more objective, but self assessments are based on people's own first-hand experience of success and failure in a wide range of everyday tasks over a long period.

Some researchers (e.g. Broadbent, Cooper, Fitzgerald and Parkes, 1982) have tried to check the validity of self assessment by having a spouse or close relative provide a parallel set of ratings. After all, your spouse is probably well placed to give an objective opinion on how often you lose your car keys or forget the shopping. In fact, self ratings have been found to correlate well with assessments made by a spouse or relative. We can be reasonably confident that properly designed questionnaires provide fairly accurate information. They also reveal clearly that memory is not just 'good' or 'bad' overall. A person's memory has strengths and weaknesses. Some people are good at remembering some kinds of things and poor at others; other people have a different pattern of success and failure. Another advantage of questionnaires is that they can be used to explore not only differences between individuals but also differences between groups. The effects of brain injury, age-related changes and sex differences can be studied by analysing the responses of different groups. For example, in a study by Cohen and Faulkner (1984) elderly people rated themselves better than young people at remembering appointments but poorer at remembering names. Sunderland, Harris and Baddeley (1983) found that people who had suffered head injuries reported more difficulty in recognizing faces and in remembering stories than normal controls.

Activity
Answer the self-rating questions on page 20 to assess your own memory. Jot down the rating values you would give yourself for each question on a piece of paper. Then show the questionnaire to a spouse/relative/close friend/colleague and ask him or her to assess *your* memory, circling the appropriate rating values. Now cross-check the two assessments and see how well they agree. If they differ, try to work out why this might be.

2.2   Knowing what you know

By and large, most people know what they do know and what they don't know. This may seem obvious, but is in fact one of the most remarkable features of the human cognitive system. Given the enormous range and quantity of information that an adult accumulates and stores over a lifetime, it is surprising that when we are asked a question we can usually say with reasonable confidence whether the answer is in store or not. Paradoxically, we know whether the search for the answer will be successful *before* it has begun.

Often, however, it turns out that there are not just two alternatives — either giving the correct answer or not knowing. There is a *gradient of knowing*. This is nicely exemplified in the TV programme 'Mastermind', in which several kinds of permitted response reflect this gradient of knowing. Suppose, for example, the question posed is 'Who was the composer of the opera Don Giovanni?' Several different states of mind and several different response patterns are possible.

1 Definitely known — a fast correct response (Mozart).
2 Definitely not known — a fast response of 'Pass'.
3 Probably not known, or if known very difficult to retrieve — there is a pause for search, followed by a slow response of 'Pass'.
4 Possibly not known but related information is available — this may produce a plausible guess which may turn out to be correct or not.
5 Thought to be known but actually not known — a completely wrong answer is given.
6 Thought not to be known but actually is known — the contestant passes but recalls the answer later.

What processes might underlie these responses? The correct answer in case 1 may be retrieved by consulting a list of composers of opera stored as part of your general knowledge, or by retrieving the memory of a particular visit you made to the opera and remembering the name seen on the programme. The 'definitely not known' response may arise if a rapid scan of memory shows that no opera composers are listed, and there is no record of any visits to the opera. There are some topics we know we know nothing about so that we hardly need to search at all. In cases 1 and 2 metamemory is accurate. The contestant knows what he or she knows or does not know. Uncertain knowledge states like 3 and 4, or outright failures of metamemory like 5 and 6 are less frequent, but can arise when information is in the store but is labelled wrongly or ambiguously so that it is difficult to find. Or the information may be labelled correctly but be so seldom retrieved that it has slipped to the bottom of the file.

It is easier to know what we know when the required fact is directly *pre-stored* in memory. But when a fact is not directly pre-stored, it may still be *computable*. This means it is possible to figure it out indirectly from other facts that are stored. For example, suppose the information 'Mozart is the composer of Don Giovanni' is not pre-stored as such, the correct answer to the question may nevertheless be computed from two other related facts, 'the composer of Don Giovanni died young' and 'Mozart died young'. In this case, the answer has to be inferred rather than being output directly. As a result, computable information generally takes longer to retrieve than pre-stored information, and may give rise to greater uncertainty.

An experimental exploration of metamemory by Lachman, Lachman and Thronesberry (1981) is described in Techniques Box B. This is an example of a naturalistic experiment. It was carried out in laboratory conditions but examines knowledge acquired outside the laboratory in everyday life. You can work through the examples as you read it.

This kind of experiment shows that metamemory is generally accurate. Most people are able to direct memory search effectively and not waste time and effort on unproductive searches. These results provide objective evidence that people really do 'know their own memories', and we can therefore feel more confident that question-naires and diaries are giving us an accurate picture of how memory functions in everyday life.

TECHNIQUES BOX B

Lachman, Lachman and Thronesberry's
Metamemory Experiment (1981)

Rationale
The experiment demonstrates that when people don't know a particular fact they can estimate accurately how close they are to knowing it.

Method
The experiment was divided into three phases.

Phase 1: Question answering   Subjects had to answer 190 general knowledge questions covering current events, history, sport, literature, etc. Instructions were: Do not guess; give the answer or respond 'don't know' as fast as possible. Time to respond was measured.

Try answering these examples of the questions yourself:
(a) What was the former name of Muhammad Ali?
(b) What is the capital of Cambodia?

Phase 2: 'Feeling of knowing' judgements   Subjects were re-presented with all the questions to which they had responded 'don't know' and asked to make a 'feeling of knowing' judgement by ticking one of the following alternatives for each question.

If you don't know the answer to questions (a) or (b) or both, tick the alternative that corresponds to *your* 'feeling of knowing'.

Definitely do not know	(1)
Maybe do not know	(2)
Could recognize the answer if told	(3)
Could recall the answer if given hints and more time	(4)

Phase 3: Multiple choice and confidence ratings   After a short delay subjects were presented with a multiple choice of four alternatives for each of the questions to which they had responded 'don't know' and

---

had to select one of these and give a confidence rating for the correctness of the choice. Values 1–4 reflect increasing confidence.

Tick which you think is the capital of Cambodia.

Angkor Wat
Phnom Penh
Vientiane
Lo Minh

Indicate whether this is:

A wild guess   (1)
An educated guess   (2)
Probably right   (3)
Definitely right   (4)

Results

1 The probability of picking the correct answer in Phase 3 increased proportionately with the strength of the 'feeling of knowing' estimate in Phase 2 (see Figure 1.2) — people who ticked (3) or (4) in Phase 2 were more likely to choose the right answer (Phnom Penh) and give a high confidence rating in Phase 3.

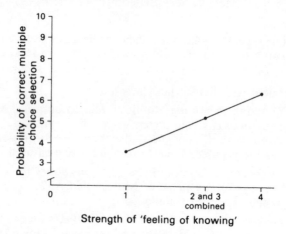

Figure 1.2 Metamemory accuracy: probability of correct recognition as a function of subjective feeling of knowing (adapted from Lachman, Lachman and Thronesberry, 1986, p. 547)

2 Response times in Phase 1 were also systematically related to the 'feeling of knowing' in Phase 2 (see Figure 1.3). Subjects searched longer for the items they (mistakenly) thought they might know (F of K values 2, 3 and 4) and terminated the search sooner for items they felt they definitely did not know (F of K value (1)).

3 Confidence ratings in Phase 3 accurately reflected the correctness of the choice. Subjects knew whether they had picked the right answer or only guessed.

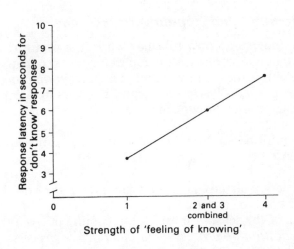

Figure 1.3 Metamemory efficiency: time taken to respond 'Don't know' as a function of subjective feeling of knowing (adapted from Lachman, Lachman and Thronesberry, 1986, p. 547)

Summary of Section 2

● Questionnaires which ask people to rate their own memory ability for different kinds of information show that memory is not good or bad across the board. People rate themselves as good at remembering some kinds of things and poor at remembering others.
● Experimental studies of metamemory show that people are quite good at knowing what they know. Knowledge is not simply present or absent. There is a gradient of knowing that reflects how easily and accurately a given piece of knowledge can be retrieved.

3 *Schema theory and everyday memory*

It is obvious enough that we do not remember all of our experiences in everyday life, and the memories we do retain are not always accurate. They may be vague, incomplete or distorted. Any theoretical approach to everyday memory must try to explain why memory works in this hit-and-miss fashion. What governs the complex pattern of remembering and forgetting? The most influential approach to this fundamental problem has come from *schema theory*. Schema theory emphasizes the fact that what we remember is influenced by what we already know.

25

3.1 'Bottom-up' and 'top-down' processing

In order to understand how schemas work it is useful to look first at an important conceptual distinction that applies to many cognitive operations. This is the distinction between *bottom-up processing* and *top-down processing*. Very many mental activities like remembering, perceiving and problem solving involve a combination of information from two sources:

1   incoming information from the outside world, i.e. the input received by the sense organs,

and

2   the information already stored in memory, i.e. the prior knowledge derived from past experience.

The analysis of the sensory information coming in from the outside is known as *bottom-up processing*, or *data-driven processing* because it relies on the data received via the senses. This sensory information is often incomplete or ambiguous, but the information already stored in the memory in the form of prior knowledge influences our expectations and helps us to interpret the current input. This influence of prior knowledge is known as *top-down* or *conceptually-driven processing*.

In practice the two sorts of processing operate in combination. For example, bottom-up processes may yield sensory information about a moving black shape of medium size and smooth texture. Top-down processes based on already stored knowledge enable this to be identified as a labrador dog. The top-down processes interact with the information provided by the bottom-up processes. This is sometimes known as *interactive processing*.

3.2   What is a schema?

The use of past experience to deal with new experience is a fundamental feature of the way the human mind works. According to *schema theory* the knowledge we have stored in memory is organized as a set of *schemas** or mental representations, each of which incorporates all the knowledge of a given type of object or event that we have acquired from past experience. Schemas operate in a top-down direction to help us interpret the bottom-up flow of information from the world. New experiences are not just passively 'copied' or recorded into memory. A memory representation is actively constructed by processes that are strongly influenced by schemas.

*The plural of 'schema' is, strictly speaking, 'schemata', but the Open Guides to Psychology use the anglicized version of the original Greek word.

   Bartlett first introduced the notion of schemas as early as 1932 in order to explain how it is that when people remember stories they typically omit some details and introduce rationalizations, reconstructing the story so as to make more sense in terms of their own knowledge and experience. According to Bartlett, the story is 'assimilated' to pre-stored schemas based on previous experience. Although for many years Bartlett's theories were rejected as being too vague, in recent years schemas have been reinstated and have a central role in theories of memory today. Modern versions of schema theory incorporate many of Bartlett's ideas, particularly the idea that what is encoded and stored in memory is determined by pre-existing schemas representing previously acquired knowledge. These schemas guide the selection of what aspects of a new input will be stored and may modify the memory representation of a new experience so as to bring it into line with prior expectations and make it consistent with past experience. New experiences in turn can be stored as new schemas or modifications of old schemas, adding to our store of general knowledge.

   Schemas, then, are packets of information stored in memory representing general knowledge about objects, situations, events, or actions. Rumelhart and Norman (1983) list five characteristics of schemas.

1   Schemas represent knowledge of all kinds from simple knowledge about the shape of the letter 'A', to more complex knowledge such as knowledge about picnics or political ideologies, and knowledge about motor actions like riding a bicycle or throwing a ball.

2   Schemas can be linked together into related systems. An overall schema may consist of a set of sub-schemas. The picnic schema may be part of a larger system of schemas including 'meals', 'outings', and 'parties'. Packets of knowledge about one topic are linked to packets of knowledge about related topics.

3   A schema has *slots* which may be filled with fixed, compulsory values or with variable, optional values. For, example, a schema for a picnic consists of slots for place, food, people, activities etc. The place slot takes the fixed value 'outdoors' (by definition) and optional values (such as woods, river, beach) can be added. The values for food, people, etc. are also optional and can be filled according to the particular occasion (see Figure 1.4). Slots may also have *default values*. That is, the schema tells us what probable values the slots can take if specific information is lacking. In the episode shown, the food has not been specified, so the schema supplies 'sandwiches' as a default value for the food slot.

4   Schemas incorporate all the different kinds of knowledge we have accumulated, including both generalizations derived from our personal experience and facts we have been taught.

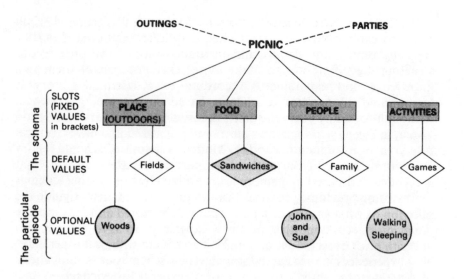

Figure 1.4 A picnic schema. The figure shows how the values supplied by a particular episode mesh with the values supplied by the schema.

5 Various schemas at different levels may be actively engaged in recognizing and interpreting new inputs. Bottom-up and top-down processes may go through repeated cycles, and the final interpretation of new inputs will depend on which schema constitutes the best fit for the incoming information. For example, if we see some people sitting on the grass we might first activate the picnic schema, but if further bottom-up information reveals banners instead of food, we might shift to the 'demo' schema instead. In this case the demo schema turns out to be the best fit and becomes the dominant or most active schema.

This list of characteristics defines a schema in broad general terms. More closely specified versions of schemas are called *scripts* (which consist of general knowledge about particular kinds of events) and *frames* (which consist of general knowledge about the properties of particular objects and locations). For the moment we can use the broader term 'schema' to cover the whole range of stored general knowledge.

3.3   How do schemas affect memories?

When applied to real-life experiences, schemas may influence memory in any of four different ways.

1 *Selection:* The schema guides the selection of what is encoded and stored in memory. Information that is not relevant to the schema that is currently the most active may be ignored. So you may not remember what clothes you wore when taking an exam, because clothes are not relevant to the activated exam schema.

2 *Abstraction:* Information in memory tends to undergo transformation from the specific to the general. So if you try to recall the occasion of a particular visit to a restaurant you tend to recall the general features common to many such visits rather than the specific details of a particular visit. Only the general schema is retained in memory, while the particular episode is forgotten. Similarly, in remembering conversations or stories you tend to retain the gist or general meaning, but not the exact wording.

3 *Integration and interpretation:* According to schema theory a single integrated memory representation is formed which includes information derived from the current experience, prior knowledge relating to it, the default values supplied by the appropriate schemas, and any interpretations that are made. The memory of a scene in a restaurant might consist of the original observations — a diner refuses a dish brought to him, and the waiter takes it away; plus the interpretation — that the customer was complaining that something was wrong with the food. This interpretation is based on prior knowledge about possible ways of behaving in restaurants, and the likely reasons for, and outcome of, such behaviour. The observations, the interpretations and the prior knowledge are integrated in the memory representation and may be impossible to distinguish later. In this way we use schema-based knowledge to infer much that is not actually seen or explicitly stated. We fill in missing information, we try to make sense of what is not readily comprehensible, we infer the reasons, causes and results of the events we witness.

4 *Normalization:* Memories of events also tend to be distorted so as to fit in with prior expectations and to be consistent with the schema: they are therefore transformed toward the most probable, or most typical event of that kind. People may misreport an event they witnessed because they remember what they expected to see rather than what they actually saw.

While the processes of selection, abstraction and normalization explain how information may be lost or reduced in memory, the processes of integration and interpretation serve to enrich and elaborate the memory trace.

3.4 Some problems with schema theory

Schema theorists are not very clear as to whether these processes (selection, abstraction, integration and normalization) take place at the time the memory is encoded, while it is in store, or at the time the memory is retrieved. Suppose your memory of a family party contains no record that a cousin was present. Did you fail to note his presence at the time, or did you excise him from the representation at some later date? Additions, deletions, interpretations and distortions may be made when the memory representation is originally constructed, or the representation may be tinkered with at some subsequent time when it is reconstructed for recall.

Schema-driven encoding and schema-driven reconstruction would produce very similar results and are therefore hard to distinguish.

Another objection is that the whole idea of a schema is too vague to be useful. A structure that is general enough to represent such a variety of different kinds of knowledge must be so unspecified that it is hard to say anything about what it is like.

Critics of schema theory also object that it over-emphasizes the inaccuracy of memory and overlooks the fact that complex events may sometimes be remembered in very precise and exact detail. Schema-driven processes of the kind described above are good at accounting for memory imperfections, but have difficulty in accounting for a memory representation that is accurate in every detail, or one that retains unusual or unexpected elements.

Another problem is that it is difficult to see how schemas are acquired in the first place. How do children manage to interpret and remember a completely novel experience when they have no prior knowledge about it, and no schema to guide the interpretations and shape the memory representations? How are schemas built up out of these unstructured experiences? The well-known child psychologist Jean Piaget devoted many years to developing a theory about how children acquire schemas. Piaget's ideas are described in Flavell (1963).

Finally, there are problems concerning the selection of the most appropriate schema. What ensures that a new input is recognized and interpreted by the right schemas? The suggestion is that those schemas that are the best match are somehow selected, but this explanation glosses over some serious difficulties.

Summary of Section 3

- Schemas are packets of stored knowledge (memory representations) derived from past experience.
- New memory representations of events, scenes and objects are the product of both stored schemas and current input.
- The bottom-up information derived from the senses about an ongoing event is interpreted by the top-down influence of relevant schemas so as to construct a memory representation that fits in with prior expectations and past experience.
- As a result, memories of particular events tend to be transformed toward a typical or 'normalized' form.

4   Memory for scenes and events

Schema theory can be best evaluated by looking at some particular studies of everyday memory. How well do people remember the events and scenes they experience in everyday life? To what extent do pre-stored schemas influence what they recall?

4.1   Remembering scenes

The influence of schemas on memory for scenes has been neatly demonstrated in an experiment by Brewer and Treyens (1981) as described in Techniques Box C.

TECHNIQUES BOX C

Brewer and Treyens' Experiment Testing Memory
for Objects in a Room (1981)

Rationale
The idea behind the experiment was that people's memory for a scene is influenced by the schema appropriate for that particular scene. In this experiment the scene was a room full of objects. Brewer and Treyens predicted that people would remember those aspects of the scene that they would expect to find in that context and forget items that they would not expect to be there.

31

Method
Thirty subjects attended one at a time to serve in the experiment. When they arrived they were asked to wait briefly in an office.

The room was designed to look like a typical graduate student's office with many of the items you would expect to find there (desk, typewriter, coffee-pot, calendar, etc.). Other items did not conform to the office schema (a skull, a piece of bark, a rolling pin). Schema-expectancy ratings for each object were obtained previously by asking 15 different subjects to rate on a six-point scale 'how likely the object would be to appear in a room of this kind'. After 35 seconds waiting in the office the experimental subjects were called into another room and given the unexpected task of writing down everything they could remember having seen in the office.

Results
Subjects did well at recalling items that had high schema-expectancy ratings (like the desk); did poorly at recalling items with low schema-expectancy ratings (like the rolling pin); and falsely recalled things likely to be in a typical office, but not actually present in this one, such as books and a telephone. Memory for the scene was therefore strongly influenced by the pre-existing schema. When they came to recall the scene subjects supplied 'default values' from the schema. Some of these were correct (the desk) but some were incorrect (the telephone).

SAQ 2
Suppose you had been in somebody's kitchen and were later asked to recall objects in it. Which of the following would you be most likely to recall? Which would you be most likely to forget?

      Cooker, sink, hat, teapot, stethoscope.

What other objects might you falsely recall having seen?

4.2 Eye-witness testimony

Eye-witness testimony has been investigated by means of naturalistic experiments — that is, experiments that try to mimic real-world situations while at the same time controlling the relevant variables. These experiments are concerned to assess the accuracy of eye-witness testimony. How accurately can people describe an event they witnessed some time previously? What factors are liable to make their reports more accurate or less accurate? These questions are not just academic. They are of paramount importance to the police and to the courts.

Much of the work on eye-witness testimony has been done by Elizabeth Loftus and her colleagues. Typical examples of her experiments are shown in Techniques Box D.

TECHNIQUES BOX D

Two Experiments on Eye-Witness Testimony

1   Loftus (1975)

Rationale
The experiment tests the theory that new information is integrated with pre-stored memory representations. Specifically, it tests whether people's memory of an event they have witnessed can be falsified if they are later given misleading information about the event.

Method
The experiment consisted of three phases:

Phase 1   150 people (the subjects in the experiment) viewed a film showing a car accident.

Phase 2   Immediately afterwards all the subjects answered ten questions about the event. Subjects had been divided into two groups, A and B. Subjects in Group A received questions, all of which incorporated accurate information about the event, and were *consistent* with what they had seen, e.g. 'How fast was the white sports car going when it passed the "Stop" sign?' Subjects in Group B received the same questions except for one which contained inaccurate *misleading* information, i.e. 'How fast was the white sports car going when it passed the barn when travelling along the country road?' (N.B. the film *had* shown the car passing a 'Stop' sign, but there was *no* barn. Mentioning a barn is misleading because it implies that there was a barn.)

Phase 3   One week later all the subjects were asked ten new questions about the accident. The final question was 'Did you see a barn?'

Results
In Group A only 2.7% of the subjects responded 'Yes' to the question about the barn.
In Group B 17.3% responded 'Yes'.
The misleading information had a significant influence on memory of the event. For a considerable number of Group B subjects, the fictitious barn had apparently been integrated with the memory representation of the filmed event.

2   Loftus, Miller and Burns (1978)

The rationale is the same as in the previous experiment.

Method
Phase 1   195 subjects viewed a sequence of 30 colour slides depicting events leading up to a car accident.
Group A saw the sequence with the upper picture in Figure 1.5 showing a red Datsun stopped at a 'Stop' sign.
Group B saw the same sequence except that it contained the lower picture showing the Datsun stopped at a 'Yield' sign.

Figure 1.5 The red Datsun at the 'Stop' sign (top) and at the 'Yield' sign (bottom) (Drawings of the photos used by Loftus, Miller and Burns)

Phase 2 Immediately afterwards all subjects answered 20 questions. For half the subjects in each group Question 17 was

'Did another car pass the red Datsun while it was stopped at the "Stop" sign?'

For the other half Question 17 was

'Did another car pass the red Datsun while it was stopped at the "Yield" sign?'

So for half the subjects the question was *consistent* with the slide they had seen and for half the subjects it was *misleading* (inconsistent).

Phase 3 20 minutes later there was a forced-choice recognition test. 15 pairs of slides were presented. One of each pair was 'old', i.e. it had been shown in the original sequence, and one was 'new', i.e. it had not been seen before. Subjects had to select the 'old' slides. The critical pair of slides showed the 'Stop' sign and 'Yield' sign.

Results
75% of the subjects who had received consistent information in Phase 2 chose the correct slide (i.e. the one with the sign they had seen in the original sequence).

Only 41% of the subjects who had received misleading information were correct (that is, 59% chose the sign mentioned in the question although it was *not* the one seen in the original sequence).

A further experiment showed that if Phases 2 and 3 were both delayed for one week, and administered so that the misleading information came just before the test, then accuracy in the misleading condition fell to 20%. Note that in Loftus (1975) false information was *added* to the memory representation. In Loftus *et al.* (1978) the correct information was *deleted* and *replaced* by the false information.

SAQ 3
In another Loftus experiment, subjects watched a film of a car accident. Subjects in Group A were then asked, 'What speed was the car travelling when it smashed into the other car?' Group B were asked, 'What speed was the car travelling when it bumped into the other car?'. Would both groups be likely to give similar estimates of the speed? If not, which group might give a higher estimate? Why?

Loftus interprets these findings as showing that the memory representation of an event can be modified by subsequent information. She claims that this new information is incorporated into the memory, updating it, and erasing any of the original information that is inconsistent with it. According to Loftus, once the new misleading information is integrated into the original memory the subject cannot distinguish its source. He or she actually believes that the non-existent barn or the non-existent 'Yield' sign was seen in the slides.

But witnesses cannot always be misled so easily. Further experiments (e.g. Loftus, 1979) have revealed conditions which make the original memory more resistant to distortion. Integration does not occur if the misleading information is 'blatantly incorrect'. In one experiment, subjects saw colour slides showing a man stealing a red wallet from a woman's bag. When asked questions about this event, 98% remembered the colour of the wallet correctly. They then read a narrative description of the event containing the misleading information that the wallet was brown. The final test showed that all but two of the subjects resisted this 'blatantly incorrect' information and continued to remember the wallet as red. Thus, memory for obviously important information which is accurately perceived at the time is not easily distorted. The colour of the wallet was correctly remembered because the wallet was the focus of the whole event, not just a peripheral detail, and its colour was correctly noted at the initial viewing. The experiment also demonstrated that once subjects recognized one piece of misleading information as false they were more distrustful and less likely to be misled by any other false information.

We can now summarize these findings. People are more likely to be misled by false information if:

1 It concerns insignificant details that are peripheral to the main event.
2 The false information is given after a delay, when the memory of the actual event has had time to fade.
3 They are not aware that they may be deliberately misinformed and so have no reason to distrust the information they receive.

So the integration of related memories is more likely to take place in some circumstances than in others. New information may be disregarded and the original memory representation may remain intact. Research on eye-witness testimony has concentrated on the fallibility of memory and so gives rather a one-sided picture. How far do the findings support the predictions from schema theory? They have often been cited as providing a demonstration of the sort of integration that is predicted by schema theory (Alba and Hasher, 1983). But it should be emphasized that Loftus' misled witnesses are not only integrating prior knowledge from internal schemas about car accidents or purse-snatching with knowledge derived from recently observed events. They are also combining information from two different external sources — an observed event and subsequent verbal information about it. Loftus herself maintains that integration takes place, with the original memory being modified by the new information, but other researchers such as Bekerian and Bowers (1983) have shown that the original memory may remain unintegrated, and, given the right circumstances, can be elicited intact. However, the eye-witness testimony findings do show that memories are not just copies of events, but may sometimes be composites based on different sources of information.

Finally, a general point should be noted. An 'update and erase' mechanism whereby schemas can be modified in the light of new knowledge can sometimes introduce errors into memory, but it can also be a useful element in a knowledge storage system. Whether or not it is an advantage depends on the type of information you want to remember. For general world knowledge it is efficient for stored facts to be updated, corrected, modified or erased. We often need to do this when we find out that facts we have stored are incorrect. But memories of personal experiences are a different matter. It may be more useful to retain an accurate recollection of personal experiences just as they actually occurred.

Summary of Section 4

● When people remember a particular scene they are influenced by the schema appropriate for that type of scene. They remember things that fit the schema and forget the things that don't.

● Experiments on eye-witness testimony show that the memory of an event that was witnessed can be falsified if misleading information is presented later.
● It is not clear whether the original memory of the event is changed or whether it is superseded by a new, inaccurate memory representation.

5   *Absentmindedness and confusions*

We have already seen that we can learn a lot about memory by studying the kind of mistakes that we make. Some of these mistakes arise out of confusions between memories of events that really happened and memories of thoughts, plans and intentions.

5.1   *Slips of action*

Everyday memory does not only consist of a record of past events. As well as remembering what has happened in the past we also use memory in everyday life to remember *plans*: to keep track of ongoing actions and of the actions we intend to carry out in the future. Failure to keep track of these plans, is usually called absentmindedness and gives rise to slips of action.

Questionnaires may be used to study absentmindedness with questions like 'How often do you go into a room to do something and forget why you went?' or 'How often do you forget whether you have done something like locking up or switching off the lights so that you have to go back and check?'

Another method which also relies on self assessment is the diary study. Reason (1979) asked 35 volunteers to keep a diary record of 'slips of action', a term he gave to unintended or accidental actions. In two weeks the diaries yielded 400 of these slips which Reason divided into five categories.

1 *Storage failures:* Forgetting that an action has already been performed and repeating it, e.g. 'I started to pour a second kettle of boiling water into the teapot, forgetting I had just filled it'. (40% of slips were of this kind.)
2 *Test failures:* Forgetting the goal of a sequence of actions and switching to a different goal, e.g. 'I intended to drive to one place but then I "woke up" and found I was on the road to another different place', or 'I went upstairs to fetch the dirty washing and

came down without the washing having tidied the bathroom instead'. (20% of slips.)

3 *Subroutine failures:* Component actions of a sequence are omitted or wrongly ordered e.g. filling the kettle but failing to switch it on; putting the lid on a container before filling it. (18% of slips.)

4 *Discrimination failures:* Confusing the objects involved in actions, e.g. taking a tin opener instead of scissors into the garden to cut flowers. (11% of slips.)

5 *Program assembly failures:* By a 'program' Reason means a set of actions linked in a sequence and directed toward a particular goal. A program assembly failure means wrongly combining actions from different sequences, like the woman who reported throwing her earrings to the dog and trying to clip dog biscuits on her ears. (Reason classified 5% of the slips as being of this type.)

The remaining 6% of the slips were unclassifiable.

You may think that some of these categories are not very clearly distinct ((4) and (5) seem very similar), and the reported percentages may be misleading. A particular kind of slip may be reported as more frequent because it is more disruptive and therefore more noticeable.

SAQ 4
Which of Reason's categories do the following slips of action belong to? Explain why.
(a) Pouring tea into the sugar bowl instead of a cup.
(b) Sealing an envelope before putting the letter inside.
(c) Cleaning teeth instead of putting on lipstick.

The important finding is that slips of action mainly occur with highly practised, over-learned routine activities. These highly practised actions become *automatic* and are carried out according to pre-set instructions with little or no conscious monitoring. Automatic actions differ from *attentional* actions which are under moment-to-moment control by a central processor which monitors and guides the sequence. A good example of this distinction between *automatic and attentional processes* occurs when you are driving a car. Emerging from a road junction is (or ought to be) an attentional process. The traffic must be scanned, distances and speeds assessed, and the driver is consciously thinking about the situation and about the decisions he or she is making. For the practised driver, changing gear is an automatic process. The actions involved do not need to be consciously monitored, and can usually be carried out successfully while the driver is attending to something quite different, like chatting with a passenger or thinking about a problem.

Automatic action sequences have the advantage that they can be carried out while conscious attention is freed to engage in some other parallel activity. However, automatization may lead to errors. An action sequence (or program) that is in frequent use is 'stronger' than one that is used less often. There appears to be a tendency for a stronger program to take over a weaker program, particularly if they share component stages. Slips of action like those Reason describes often occur at junctions between stages when there is a switchover to the wrong program. William James (1890) describes a 'strong habit intrusion' of this kind in the case of someone going to the bedroom to change their clothes, taking off one garment and then getting undressed and going to bed. The 'going to bed' program took over from the 'changing clothes' program because both shared the common action of removing the jacket. Besides strong habit intrusions, slips result from losing track of the sequence, with the effect that actions may be omitted or repeated or there may be cross-talk between two concurrent action sequences. Some individuals are much more prone to make these kinds of errors than other people, but everybody finds that slips of action increase with tiredness and stress.

Verbal slips like spoonerisms or saying one word when you meant to say another, are perhaps more common than action slips and can be categorized and explained in the same sort of way.

Norman (1981) has outlined a theoretical explanation based on schema theory for absentminded slips of action. In his model, action sequences are controlled by schemas. These schemas are knowledge structures representing information about motor actions, just as other schemas represent knowledge about places like offices or events like picnics. Several action schemas may be operative simultaneously, and are linked into related sets. The highest level 'parent' schema corresponds to the intention or goal (like 'going to work'). Subordinate 'child' schemas or sub-schemas correspond to the component actions in the sequence (like 'getting the car out', 'filling up with petrol'). Each schema has its own activation level determined both by external events (the current situation) and internal events (plans and intentions). Each schema also has a set of triggering conditions. A given schema operates when the activation level is sufficiently high, and the current situation matches the triggering conditions. So, in my example, the intention to go to work activates the whole set of goal-related schemas and approaching the filling station might constitute one of the triggering conditions for initiating the petrol-buying sub-schema.

Slips of action may occur, according to Norman's model, as a result of faulty specification of the overall intention, faulty activation of the schemas or faulty triggering. So schemas associated with very strong habits (like going to bed in William James' anecdote) may capture the action sequence because they have higher levels of activation than the schemas linked to the original intention (the 'changing clothes' schema).

Reason's test failures and program assembly failures are obviously very similar to Norman's idea about faulty triggering. In Reason's example, the triggering conditions encountered on going into the untidy bathroom set off the 'bathroom tidying' schema in place of 'fetching the washing'. Like Reason's categories of slips, Norman's causes of errors are also not very distinct. Driving to the wrong destination may be partly due to inadequate specification of the intention, partly because the activation level of the schema for taking the unintended route is particularly high, and partly because the triggering conditions are appropriate for more than one schema. It seems likely that slips may originate from a combination of all three causes. We noted earlier that a general problem with schema theory concerns the mechanism for selecting the correct schema. Norman's model for slips of action suggests how this mechanism might work and why it sometimes goes wrong.

5.2 Reality monitoring

People have two different kinds of memories. Externally derived memories are the products of actual experiences; internally generated memories are the products of thinking, imagining and planning. *Reality monitoring* is the name given (Johnson and Raye, 1981) to the ability to detect whether a particular memory originated in the world or in the head — in effect, the ability to distinguish between fact and fantasy, between a memory of an event that was actually experienced, and a memory of an event that was only imagined.

A breakdown in reality monitoring is a major symptom of schizophrenia, but do normal people actually have any difficulty in reality monitoring? Although reality monitoring is usually very effective most of us have had the experience of saying to ourselves something like 'Now I know I thought that I must remember to lock the door, but did I actually do it?' Or we find we have put the salt in the soup twice over, or not at all, because we could not remember whether we had already done it or only planned to do it. This uncertainty reflects a failure of reality monitoring, which is not always perfect. Some of the slips of action that were described in the previous section involve lapses of reality monitoring.

The type of slip that Reason called a 'storage failure' (where someone forgets they have already done an action like filling the teapot and does it all over again) occurs because the external memory of performing the action is confused with the internal memory of planning to do the action. Similarly, we sometimes mislay an object because we believe that we put the object in a certain place when in fact we only intended to do so; or we think we have told somebody something although we never did so. The memory of the planned act is mistaken for a memory of a real act. Occasionally we confuse something that happened in a dream with something that really occurred. Sometimes we use our imagination to embroider stories about things that have happened to us and cannot afterwards distinguish the fact from the fantasy.

Marcia Johnson (1985) has studied the mechanisms that underlie these confusions. Schema theory holds that memory representations of real experiences are the joint product of information derived from the external world and information derived from pre-existing internal schemas so it is not surprising that confusions do arise. How can we distinguish 'real' externally derived memories from ones that are wholly internally generated? According to Johnson's model, the two kinds of memories differ in the extent to which they have various attributes. A memory of a real event (like really locking the back door) will comprise sensory information, such as the noise of the key turning and the colour of the paint on the door, and contextual information about the time and place — where and when the action occurred and what other actions preceded and followed it. It should usually be possible to distinguish between memory traces of real events and memory traces of imagined or planned events, because the real ones will contain a higher proportion of sensory, spatial and temporal information and be richer in detail. Internally generated memories lack these details and tend to be more 'schematic'.

SAQ 5
Suppose you remember an event and cannot recall whether it occurred in a dream or really happened. How would you try to decide?

Confusions or failures of reality monitoring in everyday life tend to be associated with often repeated actions. When actions are repeated many times they become 'automatic', and in performing automatic actions we fail to attend to and encode perceptual information. Thus the memory traces of these automatic actions lack the rich sensory details that should characterize a real memory trace. For these often repeated actions, traces of the real act may not be distinguishable from traces of the imagined act. We already noted in Section 5.1 that slips of action are most common when the actions are automatic ones.

It follows from Johnson's model that if the memory of something that has been imagined is unusually vivid and rich in sensory and contextual detail it should be more difficult to discriminate this imagined memory from a real memory. An experiment by Johnson, Raye, Wang and Taylor (1979) tested this prediction.

TECHNIQUES BOX E

A Reality Monitoring Experiment by Johnson *et al.* (1979)

Rationale
People who are especially good at forming vivid and detailed visual images should be more likely to have difficulty in reality monitoring because the vividness of their self-generated internal images makes them more similar to externally derived memories. People who are poor at imagining should be better able to distinguish their vaguer images from real memories.

Method
Subjects were divided into good and poor imagers on the basis of a test requiring them to recall visual details of pictures they had seen. High scorers were classed as good imagers and low scorers as poor imagers. The two groups were shown pictures of common objects. Interspersed with the pictures were trials in which they were given the name of an object and told to imagine it. The number of times a particular picture was shown and the number of times it was imagined was varied. Subjects were later asked to judge the number of times each picture had been actually seen (ignoring the number of times it had been imagined).

Results
For good imagers, their judgement of how many times they had seen a particular picture was affected by the number of times they had imagined it (i.e. they could not distinguish clearly between memories of seeing an object and memories of imagining it). Poor imagers were less affected.

Conclusion
The greater confusion between perception and imagination for good imagers compared to poor imagers was due to the greater similarity of their imaginations to their perceptions.

5.3 Confusing implications and assertions

Besides confusing actions that were planned with actions that were performed, and visual perceptions with visual imaginings, we also make similar confusions about the verbal information we receive.

A common form of confusion occurs when people make what are called *constructive errors* in the recall of verbal information. When information is comprehended and stored in memory, the memory representation includes what was directly asserted as well as additional information that is generated from pre-stored schemas. People later fail to remember what was actually asserted (the external source) and what was only implied and then constructed internally. So sentences like —

1 *The housewife spoke to the manager about the increased meat prices.*
2 *The paratrooper leaped out of the door.*

may be remembered as:

3 *The housewife complained to the manager about the increased meat prices.*
4 *The paratrooper jumped out of the plane.*

(Harris and Monaco, 1976).

The new bits that have appeared in (3) and (4) are called '*pragmatic implications*'. The statement that the paratrooper leaped out of the door *implies* that he was jumping out of a plane. Schemas about what paratroopers normally do supply this information. People elaborate the information they receive by making inferences of this kind and cannot afterwards distinguish between what was explicitly stated and what was implied. If the inferences drawn are not correct (e.g. if the housewife was in fact only chatting and not complaining) an inaccurate memory is stored.

Harris (1978) ran an interesting experiment to investigate how the members of a jury may be influenced by pragmatic implications, and believe that something which has only been implied has actually been asserted as definitely true.

TECHNIQUES BOX F

Harris' (1978) Experiment on Courtroom Testimony

Rationale
Harris tried two ways of making people less inclined to believe that something had been asserted as true when it had only been implied. One was to instruct them not to confuse implications with assertions, and the other was to let them confer together like a real jury in the hope that at least one of the group would detect the implications.

Method
72 subjects listened to a simulated courtroom testimony lasting five minutes. Subjects were told to pretend they were members of a jury. They should listen to the evidence and would be asked questions. Half the subjects had no further instructions. Half were told to be careful not to be influenced by implications but only by the facts and were given detailed examples of how beliefs can be affected by implications. In the testimony some of the information was expressed as direct assertions and some was only implied. Subjects heard different versions of the testimony. For example, some of the subjects heard a version with the direct assertion 'I rang the burglar alarm in the hall', and some heard a version with the statement 'I ran up to the burglar alarm in

---

the hall', which implies that the alarm was rung but does not actually say so. After hearing the testimony, subjects were asked to rate 36 test statements as true, false or of indeterminate truth value. Some subjects worked on their own; others worked together in small groups.

9 of the statements had been in the testimony as direct assertions. (Assertions)
9 of the statements had only been implied. (Implications)
9 of the statements were contradicted by the testimony. (False)
9 of the statements were of indeterminate truth value.

For the test statement 'I rang the burglar alarm in the hall' subjects should have responded 'True' if they had heard the version of the testimony in which it was asserted. If they had heard the implied version they should have judged the truth value as indeterminate.

Results
The mean percentage of 'True' responses to Assertions and Implications are shown in the table.

	Groups	
	No instructions	Instructions
Assertions judged as 'True' (correct)	87.6	80.2
Implications judged as 'True' (incorrect)	67.3	60.4

Altogether 64% of the Implications were incorrectly judged 'True'. Moreover the instructions failed to reduce the number of 'True' responses to Implications by a significant extent. When subjects were allowed to make their decisions in small groups, there was also no significant improvement in accuracy.

Harris concluded that it is dangerously easy to mislead juries into believing that what is only implied is true. In his experiment subjects assumed that someone running up to a burglar alarm would ring it. An implication of this kind is incorporated into the memory representation and afterwards the information that was *heard* and the information that was *thought* (i.e. the implication) cannot be distinguished.

These results demonstrate integration of information from the senses with information derived from inferences based on the prior knowledge of what is likely to occur. Just as predicted by schema theory, it is often impossible to identify the original source of information in the memory representation. This failure to distinguish between internally derived information and externally derived information is similar to the failures of reality monitoring discussed in Section 5.2.

Summary of Section 5

- Absentminded slips of action occur when the schema for the wrong action sequence is activated instead of the schema for the correct action sequence.
- Reality monitoring is the ability to distinguish between memories of events that really happened and events that were only imagined, planned or thought about.
- Failures of reality monitoring occur occasionally in everyday life, and can be induced in laboratory experiments.
- In accordance with schema theory, confusions are due to integration. Sensory information derived from real events and from previously stored knowledge is amalgamated and may sometimes become indistinguishable.
- In remembering verbal information, facts that were only implied (and are not necessarily true) may be confused with facts that were actually stated.

6   Autobiographical memories

The study of *autobiographical memory* is concerned with how well people can remember personal experiences and events from their past, and focuses on questions such as: What kind of events are remembered best? Do memories change over time? How do we search for and retrieve these memories?

6.1   Episodic and semantic memories

Marigold Linton (1982) undertook a systematic six-year study of her own memory. Every day she wrote on cards a brief description of at least two events that occurred on that day. Every month she re-read two of these descriptions, selected at random from the accumulating pool, and tried to remember the events described, to estimate the order in which they had occurred and the date of each event. She also rated each event for salience (importance) and for emotionality, both at the time of writing the description and again at the time of recall.

To give an idea of how it worked here is an example. If I were following Linton's procedure I would record 'Took the car into the garage for service' and 'Went to a drinks party given by some new friends' as my two events for yesterday. Both events rate fairly low in importance and emotionality. If, say, two years later, I try to remember these events and date their occurrence I doubt very much if I would remember the routine event of taking the car to the garage. I probably would remember the relatively more unusual event of the party given by the neighbours, and would be able to date this by remembering when they moved into the village.

This is more or less what Linton found. She distinguished two main types of forgetting. One common form of memory loss was associated with repetitions of the same or similar occurrences. Over time there is a decrease in the distinctiveness of these repeated events. Linton described how she regularly attended committee meetings in another town. Although the first meeting and the most recent meetings remained distinctive, the rest could not be differentiated from each other in memory.

To explain this type of forgetting whereby similar memories are confused, Linton invokes a distinction between *episodic and semantic memory* which was first put forward by Tulving in 1972. Episodic knowledge is an autobiographical record of your own experiences — the events, people, and objects you have personally encountered. Semantic knowledge consists of facts about the world in general. So you might have stored in your episodic memory personal knowledge about, for example, a particular clock in your living room at home, its appearance, habits, history, etc. You also have semantic knowledge about clocks in general, their function, mechanism, defining characteristics, and so on.

Personal episodic knowledge usually includes details about the particular time and particular place in which objects and events were experienced. This is known as the *spatio-temporal context*. General semantic knowledge is not tied to a specific context in this way. In practice, of course, the two kinds of knowledge, episodic and semantic, are very closely interrelated. There is a two-way traffic (top-down and bottom-up) between them. Semantic knowledge about clocks is built up from particular experiences with individual clocks by a process of abstraction and generalization. And when a particular clock is personally encountered, top-down general knowledge is brought to bear in recognizing it, and understanding what it is for and how it works.

Everyday memory involves both kinds of memory interacting with each other in this way. Everyday experiences are the source of general knowledge; general knowledge allows us to interpret everyday experiences.

You can see how the distinction between episodic and semantic memory is closely related to schema theory. Schemas consist of packets of general semantic knowledge. Much of the knowledge in a schema is derived from repeated episodes, and schemas are used to interpret new episodes.

How is episodic information treated in memory? There are three possibilities.

1 It may be forgotten quite rapidly.

2 A particular episode may be absorbed into semantic memory contributing to the creation of a schema. The particular details are lost and only a generalized version common to similar episodes is retained.

3 A particular episode may sometimes be retained in episodic memory and remembered in specific detail.

The main features of the episodic–semantic distinction are shown below.

	Episodic memory	Semantic memory
Type of information represented	Specific events, objects, places and people	General knowledge and facts about events and objects
Type of organization in memory	Chronological (by time of occurrence) or spatial (by place of occurrence)	In schemas (packets of general knowledge relating to the same topic)
Source of information	Personal experiences	Abstraction from repeated experiences Generalizations learned from others
Focus	Subjective reality (the self)	Objective reality (the world)

This distinction between episodic and semantic memory is not accepted by all psychologists, but it nevertheless proves useful in interpreting many aspects of memory.

Now let's get back and see how this applies to Marigold Linton's trips to attend her meetings. The first trip is a novel episode and generates a lot of episodic information specific to that particular trip. It also utilizes knowledge from semantic memory. Pre-existing schemas relating to airports, taxis, hotels, committee meetings, supply basic frameworks for storing episodic information about the current event such as the names and faces of fellow committee members, the agenda, and discussion. With repeated occurrences of the meetings there is an increase in general semantic knowledge about them. The elements and patterns that are common to all meetings of that committee are abstracted and absorbed into an expanded general schema which is re-used for each event repetition. As shown in Figure 1.6, the proportion of specific episodic information distinctive to a particular occurrence shrinks and the proportion of semantic knowledge expands as the number of repetitions increases. Thus it gets more and more difficult to remember one particular occasion in a succession of repeated events. This type of confusion occurs because there is an integration of different episodes into a general memory schema.

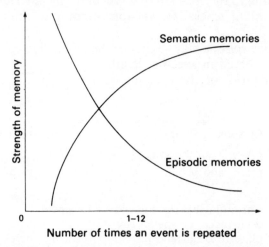

Figure 1.6   The effect of the number of times an experience is repeated on episodic and semantic memory (adapted from Linton, 1982, p. 80)

SAQ 6
Decide which of the following can be classified as episodic knowledge and which as semantic knowledge. Explain the reasons for each classification.
(a) It is possible to get from an airport to a hotel by taxi or bus.
(b) At the last meeting the chairman of the committee wore a striped tie.
(c) At committee meetings the members sit around a table.
(d) After the meeting the committee members went to eat at a Chinese restaurant.

Linton's findings that for repeated events like attending meetings she had only a general composite memory and could not recall specific dates and occasions is an example of one type of forgetting, the confusion of similar memories. She also noted a second type of forgetting. When she read the descriptions of some events, she could not remember the event happening at all. Here it is not the case that two or more similar events are confused, but that a single event is simply forgotten. For example, I may fail to remember cutting my finger two years ago. These forgotten events tend to be relatively trivial ones. Linton found that the number of events forgotten in this way increased steadily with each year that elapsed since their occurrence. For recent memories, the two types of forgetting (failure to distinguish between similar events and failure to recall) occurred about equally often, but for events that happened more than two years previously simple recall failure became increasingly frequent. By the sixth year of the study, 30% of the events recorded had been totally forgotten.

A surprising feature of Linton's study is her failure to find any strong relationship between rated importance and emotionality, and subsequent recall. Common sense experience suggests that we remember important events, or events that roused passions, better than those that were trivial or left us unmoved. However, Linton found that the emotionality and importance ratings she gave to an event initially did not correspond closely with the ones given later. She suggests that events which seem significant when they occur turn out to be unimportant with hindsight. She found it difficult to make accurate and stable judgements about the long-term significance of events, and this is probably why she failed to find a relationship between emotionality and recall. She concludes that events endure in memory if they are perceived as important and are highly emotional at the time of occurrence, and also retain the same significance later in life.

To gain insight into the way events are related and linked together in autobiographical memory, Linton has studied strategies of recall. She tried to recall all the events in a designated month. Introspective monitoring of her own recall attempts showed that many events were organized chronologically and were recalled by reconstructing events in the order they occurred. Some events were also organized in categories and were retrieved by working through named categories like social activities, sporting activities, etc. If the events to be recalled were more than two years old, there was a shift away from chronological search toward greater use of categorical search. This shift reflects the fact that time-based episodic memory representations are replaced by category-based semantic memory representations. Recall attempts also revealed that events may be organized in what Linton calls '*extendures*'. These are continuing situations such as a job or a marriage. Within these extendures specific events and episodes are embedded, and these in turn contain specific elements or details. This organization lends itself to top-down search, first accessing the relevant extendure and then homing in on a particular event.

Marigold Linton's study is a prime example of the use of the self-report method. It is also a single case study. Her findings have great intuitive appeal but obviously we should be cautious in generalizing from a single person's introspections.

6.2   Flashbulb memories

Flashbulb memory is the term that has been given to the kind of vivid and detailed recollection people often have of the occasion when they received a piece of news of public importance, such as being told of the assassination of John F. Kennedy. Brown and Kulik (1982) suggest that there is a neural mechanism triggered by events that are emotional, surprising and highly important or 'consequential'. This mechanism, they claim, causes the whole scene to be 'printed' on the memory.

Neisser (1982) has questioned this account of flashbulb memories. He believes that their durability results from frequent rehearsal and reconsideration after the event, rather than special processes activated at the moment itself. He points out that the importance of an event is sometimes not apparent at the time but is only established later. He also cites cases where flashbulb memories recounted in great detail and good faith turn out to be inaccurate when independently checked. So it is not clear whether we need to attribute the peculiar vividness and durability of these memories to some special mechanism, or whether they are just ordinary memories that survive because they are often reactivated.

Brown and Kulik base their claim that a special mechanism exists for flashbulb memories on the similarity of structure (the *canonical form*) that is exhibited. People remember where they were (Place), what they were doing (Activity), who told them (Informant), and what they felt about it (Affect). According to Neisser there is no need to postulate a special mechanism to explain these uniformities. They are the product of 'narrative conventions', the traditional schemas that govern the format for story telling. If we accept Neisser's account, schema theory can explain the canonical form of flashbulb memory. Whatever the underlying mechanism, these highly important, significant, and emotionally charged events are selectively well-preserved.

Rubin and Kozin (1984) argue that so-called flashbulb memories are not essentially different in character from other vivid memories. They asked subjects to report their clearest memories and then rate these for importance, surprise, vividness and emotionality. Amongst events recalled, accidents, injuries and encounters with the opposite sex predominated. The vividness of these memories was related to surprise, emotionality and personal importance. Although flashbulb memories are defined as relating to events of *public* importance, these *private* memories of personally important events are very similar.

Activity
Try asking one or two friends (if they are old enough!) what they remember about the occasion when they heard the news of the first moon-landings, or the assassination of John Kennedy. Do their memories conform to the typical structure? Are they especially vivid?

6.3   Remote memories

In contrast with vivid and easily recalled flashbulb memories, several recent studies have probed for more elusive and remote autobiographical memories.

One way of doing this is to ask people to recall the names of teachers or classmates from their school days. (In America this information can be verified from high school year books.) The interest of these studies lies not just in the success or failure of the recall attempts, but in the nature of the search processes. The subjects are asked to 'think aloud' as they struggle to recall the information and these running commentaries on the search process (called *verbal protocols*), provide detailed records of the way past experience is stored and organized in memory. Whitten and Leonard (1981) asked 161 university students to recall the name of one teacher from each year at school. They found that backward ordered search was more effective than forward ordered or random search. It was easier to work backwards in time than to start with the first years at school and work forwards, or just to jump about randomly. This result implies that episodic memories are not accessed independently. If they were stored and accessed independently a random order of search would be equally successful. Instead memories are interdependent, with memories that are adjacent in time sharing the same context of occurrence and being retrieved together.

In backward search the starting point is the most recent period (the last year at school) and therefore the most easily recalled. Once this is accessed it aids recall of the next-to-last item which shares some of the same context, and so on, in a reverse chaining. As Linton found (in Section 6.1) chronological ordering is a dominant aspect of the organization of autobiographical episodic memories. But search is not always chronological. The protocols also revealed that recall often involved imagery including physical attributes of the teachers ('She was a gigantic woman with a scar on her neck') and locations ('I'm thinking about which classrooms I went into'). Some teachers were remembered by the emotional responses they evoked; others were linked to important events in the life of the pupil.

Activity
Try recalling the names of *your* teachers at school. Write a short description (a protocol) of your search processes. Did you work backwards in time? Did you search locations? Why did you remember the particular names that came to mind?

51

Williams and Hollan (1981) asked four subjects between the ages of 22 and 37 to recall names of classmates. Over testing sessions amounting up to 10 hours, the number of names retrieved ranged from 83 (the poorest subject's score) to 214 (the best subject's score). Often the retrieval attempts involved recovery of locations, situations, activities, as subjects tried to generate a context within which to search for names.

> 'I'm trying to remember the name of this guy who used to — Art — he was in our 10th grade at art class — he would also bring a whole lot of people to — At his house was the first time I heard a Jefferson Airplane album.'

> 'I remember this girl who used to play the oboe, and it was junior year, she was our age — or was she older? — '

These contexts allowed the subjects to focus search on a subset of information. They often speak as if scanning internal images of scenes and events. As well as the names correctly recalled, many others proved to be incorrect. Subjects often realized this and corrected themselves.

Summing up the findings, the most striking features of these recall attempts are as follows:

1 The interconnectedness of memories: one item retrieved leads on to another. It is easier to work backwards from the present than forwards from a point in the past.
2 Subjects were able to extend their recall far beyond the limits that appeared in the initial session. Information continued to accumulate over later sessions, so persistent searching does unearth memories that initially seem inaccessible.
3 Retrieval of items from episodic memory depends heavily on re-creating the context in which the items were originally embedded. General knowledge schemas relating to activities and places (such as sporting activities, maths classes, the refectory, etc.) provide the framework for these contexts. People use general knowledge about what they did in school as a first step in reinstating specific memories.

Norman and Bobrow (1979) have developed a model of retrieval processes that fits well with the findings from these studies. They postulate three stages in the retrieval of a target item.

1 *Formation of the initial specification*. This consists of the description of the target and the context (i.e. a context-dependent description) which could be something like 'the dark-haired girl who used to sit next to me in geography'. General knowledge schemas are used to build the context-dependent descriptions.
2 *Matching a retrieved item against the specification*. An example of this process from William's and Hollan's data is: 'There was this

guy who used to sit back of me. He took Spanish classes — His last name began with an 'O' — the name Orin Elliot sticks — '

3 *Evaluation*. This stage involves judging whether a retrieved item really does fit the target specification: 'Linda Turner — that seems to fit — the last name for sure I remember'.

These three stages may be repeated in cyclical attempts at retrieval with more information being added to the target specification as further details are remembered. According to Norman and Bobrow, retrievability is a function of constructability (the ability to form an appropriate target description) and discriminability (the ability of that description to discriminate among all possible memories).

6.4   Expert knowledge

Memories of early childhood tend to be both sparse and incoherent. Relatively little is recalled of events occurring before the age of seven. This phenomenon is sometimes known as *childhood amnesia*, but we do not need to look for physical or emotional injuries to explain it. A plausible reason is that the young child has not yet developed the general knowledge schemas which are needed to interpret, organize and stabilize early autobiographical memories.

At the other end of the life span, studies of memory in old age have shown that elderly people who have a life-time of expertise in a particular knowledge domain like music or gardening have good retention of information within this domain even when memory for other matters is severely curtailed. The powerful schemas that they have developed support the retention of expert knowledge (Hulicka, 1983). Studies with adults underline the fact that it is extremely difficult to remember what you do not understand. The more you know about a topic already, the easier it is to absorb further new information about it.

The marked benefits conferred by having a rich and well-organized framework of prior knowledge have been demonstrated in experiments which compare the memory performance of 'High knowledge' and 'Low knowledge' individuals. Spilich, Vesonder, Chiesi and Voss (1979) presented subjects with an account of a baseball game. Subjects who knew a lot about baseball (the 'High knowledge' group) remembered more information than those who knew little about the game (the 'Low knowledge' group). In a similar study, Egan and Schwartz (1979) compared the performance of six skilled electronic technicians with six novices who had little knowledge of electronics, in tasks involving memory for circuit diagrams. The experts did much better at recalling meaningful (properly structured) circuits, although they were no better than the novices at recalling diagrams that were meaningless (ones that used the same symbols positioned at random). This result parallels an earlier experiment (Chase and Simon, 1973) which compared expert and novice chess players. They were asked to study the position of chess pieces on a board and later reconstruct it from memory. Experts outperformed the novices for meaningful chess positions but not for random patterns of pieces.

The benefits of expertise are also strikingly demonstrated in a study by Chi (1978) in which children who were good chess players had much better recall of chess positions than adults who were novice players. In all these experiments, expert knowledge produces better recall for material that is related to the knowledge domain and is consistent with the rules and structural regularities of that domain. With material that lies outside this domain, or that fails to conform to the legal patterns, experts do no better than novices.

High knowledge individuals do better with material within their own domain of expertise because they can map new information on to the well-developed knowledge structures (the schemas) they already possess. From their knowledge of the constraints that govern the permissible patterns, they can infer missing information or reconstruct from partially recalled information. They can also group elements of the to-be-remembered material into higher order labelled chunks, thereby economizing on memory capacity. For example, in recalling a recipe an expert cook might chunk and label one whole sequence of steps as 'prepare the béchamel', while a novice cook would need to recall each component step separately.

SAQ 7
Experimenter A compares the ability of young and old adults to recall stories and finds that old people remember significantly less. Experimenter B also compares the memory of young and old adults using different stories as test material and finds that old people do as well as or better than the young.
(a) Which experimenter used science fiction stories?
(b) Which experimenter used the plots of films from the 1940s?

Summary of Section 6

● Autobiographical memories are *episodic*. They consist of specific events, objects and people personally experienced at particular times and places. *Semantic* memory consists of general knowledge abstracted from these personal experiences and organized into schemas.

● Autobiographical memories which involve repeated occurrences of similar events become difficult to distinguish from each other.

The episodic information specific to each event is lost, while the features common to all the repeated incidents are gradually built up into general schemas in semantic memory.

- Trivial events that are of little emotional significance tend to be forgotten.
- Flashbulb memories for events that are important and highly charged emotionally seem to be recalled in vivid detail. This may be due to some special encoding mechanism or to frequent re-telling.
- Remote autobiographical memories can be retrieved by using chronological organization and searching backwards in time. Alternatively, general knowledge schemas may be used to reinstate the context of the target and generate a description of the setting, the location, associated activities, physical attributes, etc. The search process is then focused on the relevant context.
- Experts have better memories than novices because they have acquired powerful schemas relating to knowledge in their area of expertise. The schemas provide a framework for assimilating new information.

7   *Conclusions*

How does everyday memory work? Of life's rich tapestry (as the saying goes) what do we remember and what do we forget? As we have seen, there is considerable support for an explanation based on schema theory. Memory schemas, loosely defined as frameworks of prior knowledge, appear to exert a far-reaching influence on everyday memory. Schemas control and guide the implementation of plans and actions. They govern the selection of what is important to remember. The previous experience represented in schemas enables us to supply information that is missing, to make inferences, to guess what we do not know and to reconstruct what we have forgotten. Given that we cannot remember everything, schemas are a powerful device for making the most of what we do remember.

However, the benefits conferred by a schema-based memory system are also accompanied by some disadvantages. Because memories tend to be transformed toward the most probable and most familiar form, mistakes and distortions can occur. Guesses may sometimes be wrong and inferences unwarranted. When new information is integrated with a pre-existing schema it may be impossible to distinguish the old from the new. Implications are sometimes treated as assertions, and the products of imagination may be confused with real events. There is a tendency for specific details to be lost and for similar events to be telescoped in memory into a single general representation. Nevertheless, it is probably true to say that the errors that are introduced into memory by schemas are not serious enough to outweigh the advantages.

It is questionable, though, whether schema theory gives a complete account of everyday memory. Our memories of the events of our daily lives are not always so abstract and generalized as schema theory would predict. Personal episodic memories are sometimes long-lasting, detailed and accurate. We do sometimes remember what is odd or unexpected about an event as well as what is in accordance with our expectations. We may retain vivid memories of first encounters or one-off experiences when there could have been no relevant pre-existing schema to govern our remembering.

As it stands, schema theory cannot account for these facets of everyday memory, but new models are being developed to handle them. Schank (1981) has proposed a hierarchical arrangement of memory representations called MOPs, or *Memory Organization Packets*. The lowest level of the hierarchy is the most specific and representations at this level store specific details about particular events. At higher levels the representations become progressively more general and schema-like. According to the model, low-level specific memories are not usually retained for very long. As Linton found, particular event memories are absorbed into higher level generalized event memories (schemas) which store the features common to repeated experience. However, in Schank's model, details of particular events are retained if the event is peculiar or untypical in any way. So Schank's MOPs make provision for storing memories of specific episodes as well as general schemas. A model like this is clearly better fitted to account for everyday memory.

Further reading

Memory Observed by Ulric Neisser (1982) is a fascinating book. Other useful volumes are *Practical Aspects of Memory*, edited by M. M. Gruneberg, P. E. Morris and R. N. Sykes (1978) Academic Press, and *Everyday Memory, Actions and Absentmindedness*, edited by J. E. Harris and P. E. Morris (1984) Academic Press. *Memory in the Real World* by G. Cohen (1988), published by Erlbaum, provides an expanded and more up-to-date version of the topics discussed in Part 1.

Part II
Working Memory

Michael W. Eysenck

Contents

1   The memory system

Both Part II 'Working memory', and Part III, 'Encoding and retrieval in recognition and recall', of this volume are concerned with the memory system. In spite of this obvious similarity, the approach taken is rather different in each case. If one is interested in human memory, then one has to consider both the processing activities that occur at the time when memories are input and stored and those occurring at the time when memories are retrieved. Part II deals mainly with activities occurring at, or shortly after the presentation of information to the senses, whereas Part III focuses more on the ways in which information is stored and retrieved from long-term memory. Whereas Part I on 'Everyday memory' was mainly concerned with the *contents* of memory, Parts II and III focus on the *mechanisms* of memory.

While any adequate analysis of the functioning of the memory system must include a consideration of how information gets *into* the system (i.e. storage), and how it gets *out* of the system (i.e. retrieval), it is also very important to focus on the inter-relationships between storage and retrieval. As Tulving and Thomson (1973) argued, 'Only that can be retrieved that has been stored, and . . . how it can be retrieved depends on how it was stored' (p. 359). In accord with this position, storage and retrieval are treated together at several points in this Part (especially in Section 4.3), and the same is true of Part III.

One implication of all this is that Parts II and III need to be considered together in order to understand the complex workings of human memory. There is some advantage in reading the two parts in their natural sequence (i.e. Part II followed by Part III), because it corresponds to the normal sequence of events (i.e. short-term storage followed by long-term storage and retrieval).

1.1   Short-term storage of information

Psychologists have generally argued that there is a component of memory that is used for both the short-term storage of information and the active processing of information. Until comparatively recently, however, the emphasis was very much on the storage function and the component was called the *short-term store*, or *short-term memory*, and so that is where we will begin. In historical terms, the *working memory* model to be discussed later evolved out of earlier work on short-term memory.

Is this theoretical interest in short-term memory justified? We can attempt to answer this question by considering the reasons why we have a short-term storage system. Let us try to imagine the consequences of being deprived of it. Many everyday activities would become virtually impossible. For example, it would be extremely difficult to hold a conversation if you were unable to keep in mind what someone else or yourself had just been saying! In similar fashion, when thinking about some complicated problem, it is very useful to have available a short-term system that will store information about part of the problem briefly while you concentrate on other parts of the problem.

Activity
Attempt to work out the answers to the questions below purely by means of mental arithmetic (i.e. doing all of the workings in your head).

(1)	6	(2)	26	(3)	443
	+9		+78		+659

While you probably answered Question 1 without needing to rely on short-term storage of any part of the problem, most people find that Question 3 requires a certain amount of short-term storage of parts of the answer during problem solution. If you had to do this, can you remember exactly what information you held in short-term storage? More information about the strategies that people use in tasks like this will be given in Section 3.3. Question 2 represents an interesting 'half-way' house. Some people can answer such a question fairly directly, whereas others tackle it in two or three stages, storing parts of the answer as they proceed.

1.2   The multi-store model of memory

The first systematic attempt to incorporate the notion of a short-term store within a general theory of memory was by Atkinson and Shiffrin (1968, 1971). As can be seen in Figure 2.1, they proposed three kinds of memory store: *sensory registers*, *short-term store*, and *long-term store*.

This *multi-store* approach is discussed at length elsewhere (e.g. Eysenck, 1984) but its main characteristics will be sketched in here. In essence, it is assumed that input information is initially received by *modality-specific stores* (e.g. specific stores for visual and auditory information) which hold information in a relatively uninterpreted form for very short periods of time (not more than a second or two). These sensory stores are equivalent to the sensory register in Figure 1.

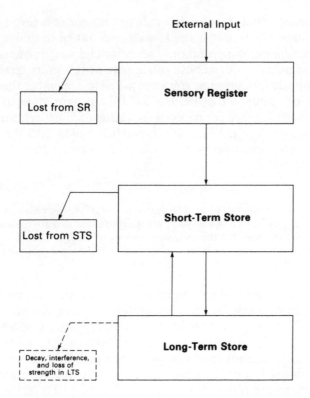

Figure 2.1   The multi-store model of memory (adapted from Atkinson and Shiffrin, 1968)

From the information bombarding the sensory stores, a small fraction is attended to and selected for further processing in the short-term store. Information in the short-term store is actively processed (typically by means of rehearsal) and may be transferred into the long-term store during the time that it is being rehearsed in the short-term store. Forgetting from the sensory store occurs by means of spontaneous decay, whereas in the short-term store items are forgotten when they are displaced from the limited capacity short-term store by new items of information coming in. Finally, it may be impossible to retrieve information stored in long-term memory because of confusion or interference among similar memory traces stored in long-term memory.

Atkinson and Shiffrin proposed a view of the short-term memory system that conforms to our commonsense intuitions in that short-term memory was regarded as being of very limited capacity and also relatively fragile (i.e. information in it could easily be displaced). Most of us probably find it quite difficult to remember a seven- or eight-digit telephone number for the few seconds taken to dial it. The fact that people can hold in mind only seven or eight digits has sometimes been taken as a direct estimate of the size of the short-term memory store. Suppose, though, that you were asked to remember the following sequence of digits: '1066193915881815'. If you noticed that the sequence is made up of the dates of the Battle of Hastings, the outbreak of the Second World War, the Spanish Armada and the Battle of Waterloo, you could probably show perfect recall of all 16 digits in the correct order.

SAQ 8
Suppose several people were asked to learn the following sequence of numbers in the order given: 14 91 62 53 64 96 48 11 00. They are told to learn the sequence with (a) no hint; (b) the rule that the sequence consists of 1^2, 2^2, 3^2 up to 10^2; or (c) the information that the entire number corresponds to the British trade deficit in 1975. Which instruction should lead to the best recall?

How, then, can we make sense of the fact that the capacity of short-term memory appears to be very variable? A classic answer to that intriguing question was provided by George Miller (1956). Basically he argued that approximately seven *chunks* of information can be stored in short-term memory at any one time. It is not easy to offer a precise definition of the term 'chunk', but it refers to any familiar unit of information based on previous learning. Thus, the sequence '1066193915881815' can be reduced to four chunks: Hastings, World War Two, Spanish Armada, Waterloo.

The Nobel-prize-winning economist and psychologist Herbert Simon (1974) tested George Miller's ideas in an experiment in which he was his own subject. He examined the capacity of short-term memory by measuring immediate memory span. This is a measure of how many items can be reported back in the right order straight after presentation, e.g. 7214568 or the words 'mind boy card egg ditto find'. His findings are shown in Figure 2.2. Memory span for words and phrases was calculated in terms of syllables and words, and produced very variable estimates.

However, Simon argued that with lists of unrelated words each chunk would consist of an individual word, whereas with lists of phrases each phrase would form a single chunk. When he calculated the number of chunks on this basis, the data began to demonstrate some consistency, and suggested to Simon that the capacity of short-term memory is approximately five chunks. The slight decrease in the number of chunks recalled as the amount of information per chunk increased may reflect the greater difficulty of rehearsing large chunks than small ones.

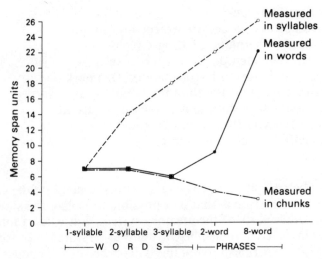

Figure 2.2   Memory span for words and phrases measured in syllables, words and chunks (Simon, 1974)

Activity

You can investigate the notion that immediate recall is limited by the number of chunks by testing your own span in much the same way that Simon did.

A list of two-word phrases and a list of eight-word phrases are given below.

1 Read each list aloud at approximately two words per second.
2 Immediately after each list attempt to recall each phrase with the words in the correct order.
3 The span measure in chunks corresponds to the number of phrases recalled completely with words in the correct order.

If Simon is right in saying that a chunk corresponds to one phrase, the number of chunks forming the span measure should be similar for two-word and eight-word phrases, provided that they are all equally familiar.

> *Two-word phrases*
> Christmas Day
> Football match
> Limited company
> Bank holiday
> Pretty Polly
> Good friends
> Coronation Street
> Closed shop

Eight-word phrases
I have nothing to declare except my genius
He goes by the name of King Creole
The evil that men do lives after them
Something is rotten in the state of Denmark
Curtsey while you are thinking what to say
Thus conscience doth make cowards of us all
What I tell you three times is true
Twopence a week, and jam every other day

The general assumption underlying attempts to measure the capacity of the short-term store is that it is possible to isolate the short-term store from other parts of the memory system. But what if long-term memory is involved in remembering items to be stored even for a very short time? An experiment to test this is described in Techniques Box G.

TECHNIQUES BOX G

Digit Span with Repeated Digits: Hebb (1961)

Rationale
Hebb tested the notion that memory span may depend in part on long-term storage of information as well as on short-term storage. He had the ingenious idea of testing digit span by presenting a series of digit strings. Some strings were repeated several times within the series. If people do, in fact, store some of the information about each digit string in long-term memory, then the repeated digit string should be better recalled than the non-repeated ones.

Method
Hebb used 24 nine-digit strings (e.g., 591437826). On each trial, one string was read aloud by the experimenter at the rate of one digit per second. The subject listened carefully, and attempted to repeat the digits in the correct order immediately after presentation. Without telling the subject, the same digit string was presented again on every third trial (3rd, 6th, 9th . . . 24th).

Results
The results are shown in Figure 2.3, which shows the number of subjects (out of forty) successfully repeating all nine digits in the correct order on each trial. The fact that the repeated string was much better recalled than the non-repeated strings indicates clearly that there is some long-term storage of digit string information. The trace of the digit string must survive in long-term memory over the intervening trials and be incremented by each repetition. So digit span is not a pure measure of short-term storage capacity: long-term memory is also involved.

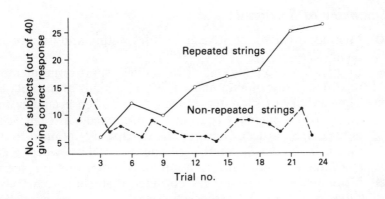

Figure 2.3 Correct digit-string recall as a function of trials and of repeated versus non-repeated strings (Hebb, 1961)

If, as Hebb's data suggest, memory span is boosted by long-term memory and so provides an over-estimate of short-term storage capacity, then this means that our short-term storage capacities are even more limited than was thought to be the case. Why is short-term storage capacity so limited? Atkinson and Shiffrin claimed that there was a short-term store with a number of 'slots' into which chunks of information could be placed, and the limited capacity was due to the small number of slots. This view ascribes the limitations of short-term storage to *structural constraints*. But why should there be so few slots? Nowadays it is more usual to relate the limited capacity of short-term memory to *processing limitations*, in particular those associated with attention. There is strong evidence that our attentional processes are quite limited in terms of the number of things or events that can be attended to at any given moment. For example, if a dangerous situation develops while we are driving, our natural tendency is to stop talking in order to devote our limited attentional resources to the task of avoiding an accident.

In the newer theoretical approach, short-term memory is essentially synonymous with the allocation of attention, and a prime function of short-term memory is to concentrate on processing important aspects of the environment. Within this viewpoint, it seems natural that the limited capacity of attention should restrict the amount of information that can be held in short-term memory.

SAQ 9
The greater knowledge of adults means that they find chunking easier than children. Would you expect children or adults to be able to hold more items in short-term memory?

Summary of Section 1

- Memory involves the storage of information and its subsequent retrieval.
- In the Atkinson and Shiffrin model, short-term memory is regarded as one of a number of different kinds of memory store.
- The capacity of short-term memory has often been assessed by means of the memory span task (i.e. immediate recall of items in the correct order). One measure of capacity obtained from this task is based on the number of chunks recalled, where a chunk is a familiar unit of information based upon previous learning.
- More recently, researchers consider that short-term memory capacity is limited by processing constraints (the allocation of attention), rather than by structural considerations (the amount of space available).

2 Components of working memory

One of the most obvious advantages of active processing and attention is its great flexibility. We can attend to people's faces, to an unusual smell, or to the text of a book. When presented with information such as 'four times five equals nineteen', we can either simply repeat it back to ourselves or engage in active processing and checking of the information presented, thus discovering that the information is false.

Baddeley and Hitch (1974) and Hitch and Baddeley (1976) were impressed by this diversity. They felt that the then-popular theoretical construct of a short-term storage system as proposed by Atkinson and Shiffrin (1968, 1971) was woefully inadequate to account for it. Accordingly, they argued that the concept of a passive short-term store should be replaced with that of an active *working memory system*. The working memory construct was clearly more complex than the theoretical view it replaced. In place of a unitary short-term store there emerged three separate components of the working memory system: a modality-free *central executive*, an *articulatory loop*, and a *visuo-spatial scratch pad*. More recently, Salame and Baddeley (1982) have suggested that a fourth component (a *primary acoustic store*) should be added to the working memory system.

A sketch map of the working memory system as it has now evolved is shown in Figure 2.4.

We can perhaps regard working memory as a hierarchical system. The *central executive* is at the top, and has a controlling or directive

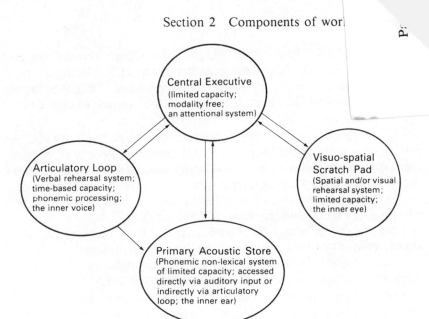

Figure 2.4   The working memory model

function over the articulatory loop, the visuo-spatial scratch pad, and
to a lesser extent the primary acoustic store. In some ways, the central
executive is the most important of these four components, since it is
used when dealing with any task of a cognitively demanding nature.
It is called the 'central executive' because it allocates attention to inputs
and directs the operation of the other components. The central
executive has strictly limited capacity, and Baddeley (1981a) suggested
that 'the central executive is becoming increasingly like a pure
attentional system' (p. 22). In other words, the central executive is a
very flexible system that can process information in any sensory
modality in a variety of different ways. It can also store information
over brief periods of time.

The *articulatory loop* can be regarded as a verbal rehearsal loop;
when, for example, we attempt to remember a telephone number for
a few seconds by muttering it to ourselves, it is the articulatory loop
that we use. The articulatory loop is also used to hold the words we
are preparing to speak aloud. It organizes information in a temporal
and serial fashion, and it deals with verbal information in terms of
its articulation. It can be regarded as an inner voice.

The *visuo-spatial scratch pad* is in some ways similar to the
articulatory loop (e.g. it can handle more than one stimulus at a time
and has the ability to rehearse information), but it deals with visual
and/or spatial information rather than the phonemic information used

by the articulatory loop. When might the visuo-spatial scratch pad be used in everyday life? One possible example is driving along a familiar road approaching a bend, and thinking of the spatial layout of the road around the bend. It can loosely be thought of as the inner eye.

Finally, there is the *primary acoustic store*. Auditory input reaches this store directly. Visual input can only enter it indirectly after being converted to phonological form (i.e. being processed by the articulatory loop). The primary acoustic store can be regarded as an inner ear.

The distinction between the different kinds of coding used by each component can be summarized as follows:

Visual code: information represented as visual features like size, shape, colour — often thought to be like visual 'images'.

Acoustic code: information represented as auditory features like pitch and loudness — a sound-based code (also called *phonemic code*).

Articulatory code: information represented as it would be spoken; similar to the acoustic code but involves the muscle movements necessary to produce sounds (also called *phonological code*).

SAQ 10
Which components of the working memory system do you think might be involved in the following tasks?: (a) listening to a story; (b) remembering a telephone number; and (c) listening to instructions telling you how to get to a particular place.

You may be thinking by now that the working memory model provides an interesting way of theorizing about the various forms of active processing we engage in, but that it would be very difficult to test it. Although there is some truth in this view, Baddeley and Hitch did manage to develop a reasonably effective methodology for testing their model.

The basic approach involves asking people to perform two different tasks at the same time. These are known as *concurrent or interference tasks*. It is assumed that every component of the working memory system has a limited capacity to process information. The rationale is that, if two tasks make use of the same component or components of working memory, then performance of one or both tasks should be worse when they are performed together than when they are performed separately. Contrariwise, if the two tasks require different components of working memory, then it should be possible to perform them as well together as separately.

2.1 Articulatory loop

We can see an example of this research strategy in operation in Techniques Box H. The issue is whether the articulatory loop is used in performing the memory span task, which was described in Techniques Box G. In this case one of the concurrent tasks is designed to use the articulatory loop. A crucial assumption is that rapid repetition out loud of something mindless such as 'hi-ya' or 'the' uses up the resources of the articulatory loop so that it cannot be used for anything else. This technique is called *articulatory suppression*. It is difficult to know whether articulatory suppression totally knocks out the articulatory loop or whether it merely uses some of its resources. In either case, if the articulatory suppression results in poorer performance on another concurrent task, then it can be inferred that this second task also employs the articulatory loop. This experimental method of concurrent tasks is a general technique for exploring the components of working memory.

TECHNIQUES BOX H

Memory Span and Articulatory Suppression:
Wilding and Mohindra (1980).

Rationale
Wilding and Mohindra used the logic just described to investigate the involvement of the articulatory loop in memory span. They examined the effect of blocking the articulatory loop with a concurrent task on memory span for letter strings.

Method
Five letters were presented visually one after the other with half a second or two seconds between each item. All subjects received some *phonemically similar* letter strings like C D E P T (the letters all sound alike) and some *phonemically dissimilar* strings like H J M R Z (the letters sound different). After a short intervening task, subjects attempted to recall each sequence of five letters in the correct order. During presentation of the letters, subjects either performed an articulatory suppression task (saying 'the the the' continuously) or they had no additional task to perform.

Results
The probability of correctly recalling the 5-letter sequences in the various conditions is shown in Figure 2.5.

Interpretation
Several points emerge from these results. It is clear that, in the 'no suppression' condition, recall of phonemically similar strings is much worse than recall of phonemically dissimilar strings. This finding indicates that both types of string are stored in the articulatory loop.

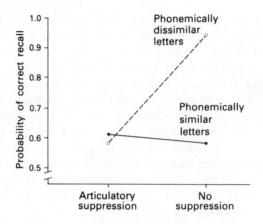

Figure 2.5   Correct letter-sequence recall as a function of phonemic similarity and articulatory suppression (Wilding and Mohindra, 1980)

Using a phonemically based system like the loop means that phonemically similar items get easily confused and are poorly recalled, but when the letters are phonemically dissimilar they are not confused and are recalled well.

With articulatory suppression, the loop can no longer function properly. In this condition, either the letter strings are still stored in the articulatory loop, but very imperfectly; or they are stored by some other component of the working memory system such as the central executive. In either case, there is no longer any superiority of phonemically dissimilar items. Memory for similar and dissimilar letter strings is equally poor with articulatory suppression. The phonemic characteristics of the letters only exert an effect when it is possible to use the unsuppressed phonemically based articulatory loop.

Additional information about the articulatory loop was obtained in several experiments by Baddeley, Thomson, and Buchanan (1975). They discovered that memory span performance for visually presented items was consistently better when short, one-syllable words (e.g. sum, hate) were presented than when the to-be-remembered list consisted of long, multi-syllable words (e.g. association, opportunity). This implied that the articulatory loop could only hold a certain number of syllables. This so-called *word-length effect* only occurred if the articulatory loop was involved. If words were presented visually and the articulatory loop was put out of action by articulatory suppression, then there was no effect of word length on span performance. Of greatest interest, Baddeley *et al.* found that in normal circumstances people can recall approximately as many words as they can read out in two seconds.

What are the implications of these findings? According to Baddeley *et al.* (1975), the articulatory loop is a time-based system that has a capacity limited to the amount a person can articulate within approximately two seconds, because any syllable has to be articulated at least once per two seconds if it is not to disappear from the store. The word-length effect occurs because the number of multi-syllable words that can be articulated within two seconds is, obviously, fewer than the number of one-syllable words that can be articulated within two seconds.

2.2   Visuo-spatial scratch pad

We have discussed the articulatory loop component of working memory at some length, and yet it is clear that it is only of use when we need to hold verbal information in storage. Much of the time, the information that we want to make use of is in a non-verbal form, often being visual and/or spatial in character. In their attempt to accommodate this fact, Baddeley and Hitch postulated a visuo-spatial scratch pad (the 'inner eye') that resembles the articulatory loop in that both hold information for short periods of time with minimal involvement of the central executive.

TECHNIQUES BOX I

Spatial versus Visual Processing: Baddeley and Lieberman (1980)

Rationale
The functioning of the visuo-spatial scratch pad is more mysterious than that of the articulatory loop, and it has proved difficult to identify its major characteristics. Baddeley and Lieberman made the important point that we should distinguish between spatial and visual processing. This distinction between spatial and visual processing may make more sense if we consider the position of people who have been blind since birth. Such people may possess accurate information about the spatial layout of objects in a room despite lacking any visual process. The possible involvement of both spatial and visual processes in memory tasks was considered by Baddeley and Lieberman.

Method
The memory task required the subject to imagine a 4 × 4 matrix. He or she was told that one particular square (the second square in the second row) was the starting square. The subject then heard a message that described the location of the digits 1 to 6 or 1 to 8 within the matrix. The digit 1 was always in the starting position, and then successive digits were placed in adjacent squares.

On some trials an easily visualized
message was presented (e.g. 'in the
starting square, put a 1; in the next
square to the left, put a 2; in the next
square down, put a 3' and so on).
This message can be visualized as
shown.

On other trials a nonsense message was presented. This was formally
equivalent to the easily visualized message except that the words 'up'
and 'down' were replaced by 'good' and 'bad', and the words 'left'
and 'right' were replaced by 'slow' and 'quick' (e.g. 'in the starting
square, put a 1; in the next square to the slow, put a 2; in the next
square bad, put a 3' and so on). These nonsense messages have to be
'translated' before they can be visualized. The easily visualized messages
contained 8 digits and the more difficult nonsense messages contained
only 6 digits. It was established that this produced a comparable
likelihood of correct reproduction of the matrix described by each kind
of message.

In order to find out whether subjects used the visuo-spatial scratch
pad with the easily visualized messages, Baddeley and Lieberman used
the concurrent task technique. There were three conditions.

1 Message Only: subjects had the task of remembering either the easily
  visualized or nonsense messages, but there was no concurrent task.

2 Concurrent Visual Task: as well as remembering the messages,
  subjects did a concurrent visual task involving brightness judgements.
  Light patches were presented every 2.5 seconds and had to be judged
  bright or dim.

3 Concurrent Spatial Task: as well as remembering the messages
  subjects did a concurrent spatial task. Blindfolded subjects had to
  try to point a flashlight at a photocell located at the tip of a swinging
  pendulum. When they were successful, auditory feedback was given.
  There were two groups of subjects: Group 1 did Conditions 1 and
  2; Group 2 did Conditions 1 and 3.

Results

	Mean number of correct reproductions (out of 8)	
Group 1		
Message	*Message only*	*With concurrent visual task*
Easily visualized	5.75	4.72
Nonsense	7.25	4.14
Group 2		
Message	*Message only*	*With concurrent spatial task*
Easily visualized	6.75	3.14
Nonsense	6.50	5.14

Thus performance with the easily visualized messages was impaired by the spatial task, whereas performance with the nonsense messages was disrupted by the visual task. None of the other differences were significant.

Interpretation
These findings clearly indicate the value of distinguishing between visual and spatial processes. In addition, as Baddeley and Lieberman pointed out, spatial processing appears to be more important than visual processing for retention of information presented in the form of easily visualized messages. They went further and proposed that the visuo-spatial scratch pad might be more a spatial than a visual system.

2.3   Primary acoustic store

The original version of the working memory model did not incorporate an acoustic or auditory store. Why has it now been decided (Salame and Baddeley, 1982) to add a primary acoustic store to the model? The reason for distinguishing between an articulatory loop (or inner voice) and an acoustic store (or inner ear) can be seen in terms of a very simple (but quite revealing) demonstration activity.

Activity
Go back to the last paragraph and read it to yourself, saying out loud 'the the the' all the time. While you do so, try to think of the sounds of the printed words as you read.

Were you able to do this? Most people can, and the fact that you can 'hear' what you are reading despite articulatory suppression suggests that the 'inner ear' can be used even when the reader is articulating something else.

Of course, it would be unwise to postulate a primary acoustic store purely on the basis of introspective evidence. More formal evidence was obtained by Baddeley and Lewis (1981). They asked their subjects to decide whether visually presented nonsense words did or did not sound like real words. Some examples are 'cayoss' and 'bambil'. Articulatory suppression did not affect performance on this task. The fact that decisions about the sounds of real and nonsense words could be made without resort to the articulatory loop suggests that there may be an acoustic code as well as an articulatory one. Articulatory suppression also failed to have much effect on another task that required subjects to read visually presented words and judge whether they rhymed with each other. So it seems that the primary acoustic store is involved in the reading process.

2.4 Central executive

The central executive is the most versatile of the components of the working memory system. It closely resembles attention, and thus possesses limited capacity, and it is of use in the active processing of information and in the transient storage of information. If we may assume that the central executive is involved in all attentionally-demanding tasks, then it follows that problem solving, reasoning, reading, mental arithmetic, learning, writing, and a host of other activities all utilize the central executive.

Sometimes the involvement of the central executive is inferred from the fact that none of the other components of the working memory system appears to be involved. For example, in Techniques Box H we saw that a certain level of memory performance in a span task was possible even when the articulatory loop was largely unavailable, and that this suggested the possible involvement of the central executive.

More direct evidence is available from comparing performance on two tasks that are performed either singly or together. This is known as the *dual-task technique*. If the two tasks are very different but nevertheless interfere with each other, then it is plausible to assume that they are both competing for the same attentional resources of the limited capacity central executive. Hunt (1980) provided a good illustration of this technique. His subjects had to perform a psychomotor task and intelligence test simultaneously. The psycho-motor task was guiding a lever between two posts with the thumb and index finger of the left hand. The intelligence test was one known as Raven's Matrices, which involve visual patterns. When both tasks were performed together, performance on the psychomotor task deteriorated progressively as the Raven problems became harder.

How should we interpret this interference effect? It seems highly unlikely that the two both make use of any of the same specific processing systems (e.g. the articulatory loop or the visuo-spatial scratch pad). Accordingly, the most plausible assumption is that they both make use of a very general processing system such as the central executive.

We have discussed the working model at some length. Of course, in order for the model to be of real use, we need to demonstrate that it can help to provide some understanding of the components involved in everyday activities such as reasoning and reading. It is to such issues that we now turn.

Summary of Section 2

- The working memory model replaces the unitary short-term store with four separate components: the central executive, the articulatory loop, the visuo-spatial scratch pad, and the primary acoustic store.
- A major advantage of the working memory model is that it treats the short-term storage of information and more general processing activities within a single theoretical framework.
- If two tasks are performed at the same time, they should not interfere with each other if they make use of different components of the working memory system. In contrast, they should interfere if they both use one or more components in common. The most commonly used techniques are articulatory suppression and the dual-task technique.
- Some of the main experimental findings can be summarized as follows:
  - (a) The articulatory loop retains verbal information and can hold about two seconds' worth of syllables.
  - (b) The visuo-spatial scratch pad appears to use spatial coding as well or instead of visual coding.
  - (c) A primary acoustic store can retain acoustic information even when the articulatory loop is blocked by articulatory suppression and is involved in reading.
  - (d) The central executive is involved in all tasks that require attention.

3   Functions of working memory

An interesting question is how the resources of the working memory system are used in the performance of intellectually demanding tasks. It seems common sense to assume that such tasks would require close attention (and thus the resources of the central executive) but the involvement of the other components of the working memory system would presumably depend on the exact nature of the task.

SAQ 11
If you tried to solve visually presented anagrams, which component or components of working memory would probably be involved?

75

3.1   Verbal reasoning problems

A task that has been studied in some detail is the *verbal reasoning task* invented by Baddeley (1968). It consists of a series of short sentences, each of which is followed by two letters (A and B) either in the order 'AB' or 'BA'. Each sentence describes the order of the two letters (e.g., 'A precedes B'), and the subject's task is to decide as rapidly as possible whether the sentence is a true or a false description of the letter pair that follows it. The complexity of the task was varied by using different sentence forms.

Activity
Cover the page with a piece of card. Do each problem in turn, marking each one T (true) or F (false). If you have a stop watch you could try to keep a record of how long it takes you to solve each one. If you cannot time yourself simply note which problems you found most difficult.

1   A precedes B: AB
2   B is preceded by A: BA
3   A does not follow B: BA
4   A is not followed by B: BA
5   B is not preceded by A: AB
6   A does not precede B: BA
7   B is followed by A: BA
8   B follows A: BA

When you have done that, check whether you have got all of the answers right: 1, 4, 6, and 7 are true, and 2, 3, 5, and 8 are false. Problems 1 and 8 use the active affirmative sentence form; problems 2 and 7 the passive affirmative; problems 3 and 6 the active negative; and problems 4 and 5 the passive negative. It is usually found that active affirmatives are the easiest, followed by passive affirmatives, active negatives, and passive negatives in that order. Is that what you found? If you managed to record times you probably found the times reflect the order of difficulty.

As you may have discovered when doing the verbal reasoning task, it seems necessary to use the attentional resources of the central executive to solve these problems, especially the more difficult ones. Since it is a verbal task, it is also possible that the articulatory loop is involved. How can we decide whether or not the central executive and the articulatory loop are involved in the performance of this task?

TECHNIQUES BOX J

Verbal Reasoning and Articulatory Suppression:
Hitch and Baddeley (1976)

Rationale
The basic strategy adopted by Hitch and Baddeley was to require their subjects to perform an additional concurrent task while performing the reasoning task. In Condition 1, the additional task was to say the word 'the' repeatedly, an articulatory suppression task assumed to involve only the articulatory loop. In Condition 2, the additional task was to say the sequence 'one two three four five six' over and over again. Since the sequence is so heavily overlearned, and thus presumably can be repeated without requiring the attentional resources of the central executive, it was assumed that this task would also involve only the articulatory loop. In Condition 3, the additional task was to repeat a different random string of six digits out loud on each trial, so this is equivalent to a memory-span task. In addition to using the articulatory loop, this task presumably requires attention and thus the central executive. In Condition 4, no additional task was used (control condition), to provide a baseline against which to measure the detrimental effects (if any) on performance of the verbal reasoning task produced by the various additional tasks.

Method
Thirty-two versions of the problems in the verbal reasoning task were devised, comprising all possible combinations of sentence voice (active or passive), affirmation (affirmative or negative), truth value (true or false), verb (precedes or follows), and letter order. Each problem was presented visually, and during each trial the subject said 'the' repeatedly (Condition 1), or 'one two three four five six' (Condition 2), or repeated a string of six random digits (Condition 3), or there was no additional task (control condition). All subjects were run in all conditions. The time taken to press the 'True' or 'False' button was recorded.

Results
Speed of performance in the verbal reasoning task in each condition is shown in Figure 2.6.
  The first point to note is that the performance was only slightly (and non-significantly) worse in the articulatory suppression conditions (i.e. Conditions 1 and 2: 'the' and 'one two three four five six') than in the control condition (4). This indicates that the articulatory loop plays little or no part in the performance of the verbal reasoning task. In contrast, the additional task that required use of the central executive as well as the articulatory loop (i.e. Condition 3: repeating a string of

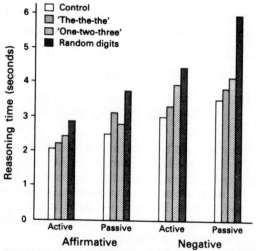

Figure 2.6   Speed of solution of verbal reasoning problems (Hitch and Baddeley, 1976)

six random digits) produced a considerable increase in response time, especially with the more complex versions of the verbal reasoning task.

Interpretation
Hitch and Baddeley interpreted these results as demonstrating that the verbal reasoning task and the most demanding additional task (i.e. six random digits) both competed for the limited resources of the central executive, and it was this that slowed performance on the reasoning task. More complex versions of the verbal reasoning task presumably required more of the central executive's resources, and so were more adversely affected by the concurrent task.

You may have noticed from the figure that the data discussed above suggest that articulatory suppression might have been affecting verbal reasoning slightly, even though the effects were non-significant. Hitch and Baddeley (1976) further explored the possible involvement of the articulatory loop for verbal reasoning in another experiment. They used the same verbal reasoning task that has already been described, but this time they varied the letter pairs. Some of the letter pairs were composed of phonemically similar (sound-alike) letters (BP; MN; FS; TD), whereas others were composed of phonemically dissimilar letters (MC; VS; OQ; XY). The key finding was that the number of verbal reasoning problems that could be solved correctly in a given time was lower when phonemically similar letter pairs were used than when phonemically dissimilar ones were used. This indicates that some phonemic (sound-based) processing must have been occurring during the reasoning task since there is no reason why letters which sound alike should be more difficult unless subjects are sounding them out to themselves. Phonemic processing has been shown to be largely a function of the articulatory loop, so it seems that the articulatory loop is used to facilitate verbal reasoning performance. In other words, while verbal reasoning primarily involves the central executive, it is likely that there is also a modest contribution made by the articulatory loop.

We have concentrated on the ways in which the performance of a verbal reasoning task is dependent on the various components of the working memory system. The general conclusion from the research discussed so far is that it is relatively straightforward to discover which components of working memory are involved in reasoning or other cognitively taxing tasks. By seeing which additional, concurrent tasks impair performance on the main task, we can build up a picture of how that task is normally approached.

As you have undoubtedly discovered already, psychology has been noted throughout its history for theoretical controversies. There are various theorists who object to the notion that there is a general, modality-free system such as the central executive which can direct attention to the needs of various tasks. They could therefore dispute the interpretation just given of the factors responsible for verbal reasoning performance. According to Allport (1980), the term 'attention' (and, thus, also 'central executive') is used in a rather vague way without any adequate specification of how it actually functions. This vagueness means that it can be used to explain almost any experimental results that are found. When two cognitively demanding tasks are performed together, disruption of performance can be 'explained' in terms of exceeding the capacity of attention or the central executive; but when there is no disruption this too can be accounted for by assuming that the two tasks do not exceed the available resources of the central executive. This line of argument, which is to be found in the article by Hitch and Baddeley (1976), is suggestive of 'Heads I win, tails you lose' and runs the danger of becoming entirely circular. Furthermore, since explanations based on the central executive are all too easy to provide, they may have the disadvantage of preventing us from examining in detail what is happening.

It is probably fair to state that Baddeley and Hitch would agree that relatively little is known of the workings of the central executive or attentional system. However, the fact that very different tasks often cause interference with each other suggests the existence of some very general processing resource such as attention or the central executive. Furthermore, theories in psychology are typically only abandoned when better theories are proposed, and it is not clear that this point has been reached as yet.

Summary of Section 3.1

● Verbal reasoning primarily involves the central executive, but may also involve the articulatory loop to some extent.
● There is controversy concerning the usefulness of the theoretical construct of the central executive and its role in directing attention.

3.2   Letter-transformation problems and mental arithmetic

In spite of the theoretical controversy concerning the explanatory status of their construct of the central executive, Baddeley and Hitch would still claim that the problems and mental tasks that we encounter in everyday life normally require the use of attentional processes of the central executive for their successful solution. It is perhaps less obvious that many of these tasks also necessitate the temporary storage of information relating to the task. This happens whenever information becomes available at one point in the solution of a problem and must be maintained for subsequent use. If there is any validity to these speculations, then this opens up the intriguing possibility that many of the limitations that seem to be intellectually based may actually be merely limitations on the short-term storage of information in working memory.

Activity

A dramatic illustration of the way in which increasing memory load can affect problem solving is demonstrated by the following *letter-transformation task*. Each of between one and four letters has to be transformed to a letter that is a specified number of places ahead in the alphabet. Thus, for example, the answer to 'G + 4' is 'K', the answers to 'LS + 4' is 'PW', and the answer to 'MSER + 4' is 'QWIV'. In this task, you are not allowed to write down any of the letters in any one answer until all of the letters in that problem have been transformed. Attempt the following problems, and ask yourself why some take much longer than others.

		Answer			Answer
(1)	C + 4		(5)	BTDA + 4	
(2)	HR + 4		(6)	HFT + 4	
(3)	JFI + 4		(7)	EO + 4	
(4)	LDGN + 4		(8)	J + 4	

The correct answers are as follows: G; LV; NJM; PHKR; FXHE; LJX; IS; N. Although the processing demands remain constant as the number of letters per problem increases (the letter transformation required is always '+4') you probably discovered that three- and four-letter problems took much longer than one- and two-letter problems. This reflects the substantial effects on problem solving of a modest memory load (after all no more than three letters ever need to be stored). As you may agree, the task is harder than it looks. I have used this task extensively and have consistently found that a small proportion of university students cannot solve any four-letter problems.

More formal evidence on the letter-transformation task was obtained by Hamilton, Hockey, and Rejman (1977). They used varying sizes of transformation (+1; +2; +3; +4) (whereas the Activity above required only transformations of +4). Their findings in terms of speed of solution are shown in Figure 2.7.

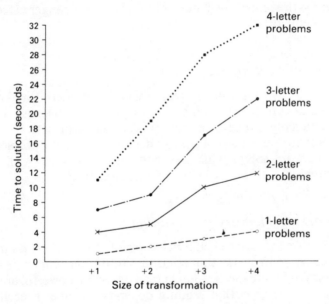

Figure 2.7   Speed of solution of a letter-transformation task as a function of number of letters and size of transformation (Hamilton, Hockey and Rejman, 1977)

While the size of the required transformation had only a relatively small impact on performance, the number of letters per problem had a marked effect, indicating that the demands for transient storage of taks information increased progressively as the number of letters requiring transformation increased. For example, in order to calculate that the answer to 'LDGN + 4' is 'PHKR', the transformation of the first letter (i.e. 'P') needs to be stored while the second letter is transformed, the accumulating answer (i.e. 'PH') must be retained while the third letter is transformed, and so on.

How is the working memory system involved in the performance of the letter-transformation task? The complexity of the task (especially when three or four letters have to be transformed) suggests a progressively greater involvement of the central executive as the number of letters to be transformed increases. In addition, the use of verbal material and the need to remember the transformed letters in the correct order suggest the involvement of the articulatory loop.

Teachers will be familiar with the frustrations often experienced by children when given mental arithmetic problems. A significant source of difficulty appears to be the demands placed on the short-term storage of information in working memory. This was convincingly shown by Wanner and Shiner (1976) with relatively simple subtraction problems — they might well have obtained even stronger effects with more difficult problems.

Summary of Section 3.2

- Many kinds of problems (e.g. mental arithmetic) make heavy demands on the working memory system because of their simultaneous processing and storage requirements.
- Apparently quite modest storage demands can make problems very difficult to solve. This has been demonstrated with mental arithmetic and the letter-transformation task.

3.3   Working memory and reading

Over the years there has been much interest in the processes involved in reading. A controversy that continues to this day concerns the role (if any) played by subvocalization in reading. Some powerful arguments in favour of the view that reading depends on inner speech or the articulatory loop were put forward by Huey (1908) in his classic text, *The Psychology and Pedagogy of Reading*:

> The carrying range of inner speech is considerably larger than that of vision . . . the initial subvocalization seems to help hold the word in consciousness until enough others are given to combine with it in touching off the unitary utterance of the sentence which they form . . . It is of the greatest service to the reader or listener that at each moment a considerable amount of what is happening should hang suspended in the primary memory of the inner speech.   (Huey, 1908, pp. 144–8)

Although the terminology used by Huey may have a somewhat dated air about it, the gist of what he has to say has a surprisingly modern feel about it. The fact that it is called inner speech appears to equate it with the articulatory loop, the inner voice where words are sounded out and prepared for speech. However, it is possible that the primary acoustic store or inner ear is also involved in the transient storage of sentence information for subsequent use.

It will perhaps come as no surprise to learn that the involvement of the articulatory loop in reading seems to depend on the nature of the reading task. After all, reading a popular novel for pleasure is a very different activity to inspecting the small print of a legal contract. Intuition suggests that we are more likely to resort to subvocalization when what we are reading is complicated, and this was confirmed in an ingenious study by Hardyck and Petrinovich (1970). They found that people tend to show increased muscle activity of the larynx when they are reading. When they trained their subjects to suppress this muscle activity while reading, there was no effect on comprehension of simple prose passages, but comprehension of complex prose suffered.

It is of particular interest to consider the effects of articulatory suppression on reading. According to the normal concurrent task rationale, if suppression of the articulatory loop does *not* hinder reading, this implies that the loop is not used in reading. Sometimes the effects of articulatory suppression are negligible or non-existent. The task of deciding whether simple sentences (e.g. *Canaries have wings*) are true or false was performed as rapidly and accurately with articulatory suppression as without it (Baddeley, 1979). However, there may be some doubts as to whether this is a proper reading task because of its simplicity. Levy (1978) investigated some of the factors determining whether or not the articulatory loop is used in reading. She discovered that reading to extract the gist was not affected by articulatory suppression. However, when subjects had to remember the exact wording of visually presented sentences, there was a detrimental effect of articulatory suppression on performance.

Baddeley, Eldridge, and Lewis (1981) also made use of articulatory suppression. They used sentences which were either meaningful or *anomalous*. An example of an anomalous sentence is: *She doesn't mind going to the dentist to have fillings, but doesn't like the rent when he gives her the injection at the beginning.* Subjects had to decide whether each sentence was meaningful or anomalous, a task that requires close attention to the individual words. Performance was adversely affected by articulatory suppression.

How can we explain the fact that in some reading tasks saying 'the the the' (articulatory suppression) has an interfering effect, but in others it does not? While we do not have a complete answer as yet, it appears that the articulatory loop tends to be used when the central executive is becoming overloaded. This is a possible explanation of the effects on reading complex prose material noted by Hardyck and Petrinovich (1970) and on the difficult task of distinguishing between meaningful and anomalous sentences (Baddeley, Eldridge and Lewis, 1981). Since the articulatory loop seems to be particularly useful at preserving the order in which verbal items are presented, it is only to be expected that it is used when the reading task requires word-for-word recall (Levy, 1978).

If the articulatory loop does play a significant role in reading, the next issue is to consider exactly how it facilitates reading. The most popular view, expressed in the quotation from Huey (1908) given above, is that the intake of visual information from the printed page leads to a verbatim record of the last few words in the articulatory loop and this record is then used in the comprehension process. There is increasing evidence that this view is profoundly mistaken, in part because it implies that comprehension is a rather slow and laborious process. Contrary evidence was obtained by Rayner, Carlson, and Frazier (1983) using measurements of eye movements. They asked people to read a sentence such as: *As she was sewing the sleeve fell off her lap.* While readers initially assumed that the subject of the sentence was the person doing the sewing rather than the sleeve, they corrected their error very quickly, as revealed by the fact that the word 'fell' was fixated for an abnormally long time. This means that the inaccurate first interpretation was detected quickly enough to affect eye movements occurring within approximately 250 milliseconds.

The most obvious problem with the notion that reading involves a sequential process of visual information intake, followed by recoding as a phonological representation in the articulatory loop, and finally comprehension, is that it seems to imply that the articulatory loop always forms a vital part of the reading process. This is, of course, refuted by the various studies in which articulatory suppression had no effect at all on reading. Perhaps the articulatory loop acts as a kind of back-up system that is used as and when a current reading task becomes too difficult for whatever reason. If the reading task is straightforward and easy, the visual information may be comprehended directly without utilizing the articulatory loop.

It is natural to wonder why the emphasis in this section on the use of working memory in reading has been so heavily on the articulatory loop component of the working memory system, especially since common sense indicates that the central executive, the visuo-spatial scratch pad, and the acoustic store may all play a part in normal reading. The reason is simply that because convenient techniques exist nearly all of the research has investigated the articulatory loop. It is especially unfortunate that so little is known of the role of the central executive and the other components but these are more difficult to investigate.

Summary of Section 3.3

- Inner speech is sometimes (but not invariably) used in reading.
- It is often assumed that inner speech is represented in the articulatory loop, which is most likely to be used in reading when the text material is difficult and/or the exact order in which verbal items are presented must be remembered.
- The evidence suggests that the articulatory loop does not constitute a vital component of the reading process; rather, it acts as a back-up system. In any case, experiments suggest that, even when the articulatory loop is largely used up by articulatory suppression, it is still possible to 'hear' the sounds of words on the page, i.e. to use the inner ear rather than inner speech.

3.4   An evaluation of working memory

Baddeley's working memory model represents a valuable contribution in various ways. There is by now almost universal agreement that it is much more realistic to assume that working memory consists of several relatively independent processing mechanisms rather than a single unitary short-term store. It also seems useful to treat attentional processes and short-term storage as parts of the same system, primarily because they are probably used together much of the time in everyday life. Finally, the notion that any one component of the working memory system may be involved in the performance of a great number of apparently very different tasks is a valuable insight. The best illustration of this notion is the articulatory loop, which has been shown to be used in memory span tasks and mental arithmetic, and, to a lesser extent, in verbal reasoning and reading.

Perhaps the greatest limitation of the working memory model is that we know least about the component that is undoubtedly of greatest general importance, the central executive. The central executive is presumably used to deal with the demands of tasks or activities, allocating attention to various aspects of the tasks, and integrating and evaluating results. For example, we may hold the results of letter-transformation tasks in the articulatory loop, but how do we know which is the correct answer?

In spite of the frequent assertions by Baddeley and Hitch that one of the major characteristics of the central executive is its limited capacity, there have never been any successful attempts to measure that capacity. A further difficulty with the central executive has been raised by Richardson (1984). He pointed out the way in which the central executive can apparently carry out an enormous variety of processing activities in different conditions. This variety poses obvious problems in terms of describing the precise function of the central executive and may indicate that the notion of a single central executive is as misplaced as the idea of a unitary short-term memory. Allport (1980) and others have suggested replacing a central allocation of attention with several specific processing mechanisms. Perhaps surprisingly, Baddeley (1981b) has himself argued for a somewhat similar position. He argued that his strategy was to identify as many specific processing mechanisms as possible (e.g. the articulatory loop, and the visuo-spatial scratch pad), thus progressively chipping away at the central executive. According to this view, the central executive can be thought of as the remaining area of ignorance.

My own opinion is that we should not abandon the notion of some general central executive. If the human mind really consisted of nothing but numerous specific processing mechanisms operating in isolation from each other, it seems likely that total chaos would result. At the very least, some central system seems to be needed in order to co-ordinate the activities of the specific mechanisms, and the central executive seems well suited to that role.

A final issue needs to be considered. How do we decide that some processing mechanism is of sufficient importance to be identified as a component of the working memory system? Consider, for example, a study by Reisberg, Rappaport, and O'Shaughnessy (1984) on what they described as the 'digit digit span' (because numbers are encoded in terms of finger movements). In essence, they taught their subjects to store lists of digits by 'typing' them on an imagined typewriter, and found that this strategy increased the number of digits which could be remembered by 50 per cent. We may be inclined to dismiss this new-found mechanism as a task-specific trick rather than as pointing to the existence of an additional component of working memory (the 'finger store'?). However, it is difficult to justify this decision within the theoretical framework adopted by Baddeley and Hitch.

4   *Levels of processing*

As we have seen, the working memory model provides us with some insights into the active processes we use in our everyday interactions with the environment. It also addresses the issue of the amount of information that can be 'held' over short periods of time in the articulatory loop. What it does not do, however, is to consider in any detail key questions about its relationship to long-term memory. For example, is information better remembered over long time intervals if it has been processed by the articulatory loop? Sadly, we do not know the answers to such questions, in spite of the fact that it seems intuitively likely that how well we remember events depends on the way in which we processed and thought about them at the time they occurred.

The fact that the working memory system permits stimulus inputs to be processed in very diverse ways suggests that it may well be fruitful to consider the effects of different processing activities in working memory on the long-term storage of information. In particular, the central executive, which can apparently be used very flexibly, deserves consideration. The nature of the information stored in long-term memory must be affected by the precise use of these attentional resources at the time of learning.

4.1   *Depth of processing*

An important approach which argued that memory traces could usefully be regarded simply as the by-products of perceptual and attentional processes was the *levels-of-processing theory* put forward by Craik and Lockhart (1972). They suggested that there is an attentional system (somewhat resembling the central executive) which can process any given stimulus in a number of different ways. If you see the word 'CHAIR', you may focus on the individual letters, on the sound of the word, or on its meaning. According to Craik and Lockhart, processing varies in terms of its depth, a notion that was defined by Craik (1973): '"*Depth*" is defined in terms of the meaningfulness extracted from the stimulus rather than in terms of the number of analyses performed upon it' (p. 48).

The crucial theoretical assumption made by Craik and Lockhart (1972) is that the depth or level of processing determines persistence of a memory trace in long-term memory. According to them, 'Trace persistence is a function of depth of analysis, with deeper levels of analysis associated with more elaborate, longer lasting, and stronger traces' (p. 675). Analysis of meaning is important for long-term retention. If a foreigner chatted to you, you would almost certainly remember practically nothing of what was said, because it would have no meaning for you. On the other hand, if an interpreter translated then it would be much easier to remember the message.

Activity

You can test the levels-of-processing theory by working through the list of words below. Try to maintain a steady rate of about one word every five seconds. Think of a word that rhymes with the list word or an appropriate adjective to go with each word, as indicated. (For example if the list word were HOUSE a rhyme might be MOUSE or an appropriate adjective would be NEW).

BOOT	(rhyme)
CARD	(rhyme)
DOG	(rhyme)
LIGHT	(rhyme)
STREET	(rhyme)
RUGGER	(adjective)
ELM	(adjective)
SKY	(adjective)
HERO	(adjective)
INK	(adjective)
BOY	(adjective)
TELEPHONE	(adjective)
BADGER	(adjective)
CHAIR	(adjective)
MACKEREL	(adjective)
WATCH	(rhyme)
BOOK	(rhyme)
CAKE	(rhyme)
SWEATER	(rhyme)
PAPER	(rhyme)

Now cover the paper and write down as many of the list words as you can remember in any order. When you have done that, add up the number of words recalled that had the rhyming task performed on them and the number that had the adjective task. Thinking of a rhyme for each noun does not require you to consider the meaning, and so processing is shallow, whereas thinking of an appropriate adjective for each noun does require you to think about the meaning, and so processing is deep. You should find that the adjective task produces better recall than the rhyme, i.e. you remember more of the adjective words than the rhyme words.

This Activity provides a simple demonstration of the major experimental technique used to study levels-of-processing theory. In essence, different tasks (often referred to as *orienting tasks*) are performed on a list of words. An attempt is made to ensure that one or more of these orienting tasks requires the processing of meaning (e.g. an adjective task), and one or more does not require that meaning be processed (e.g. a rhyme task). Craik and Lockhart (1972) argued that it is preferable for the subjects not to know beforehand that there will be a memory test (this is known as *incidental learning*), because then they will be less tempted to perform analyses in addition to those required by the orienting task. When learning is *intentional* (i.e. a memory test is expected) they may carry out extra processing in an effort to improve their performance. A well-known study examining levels of processing in both intentional and incidental learning is described in Techniques Box K.

TECHNIQUES BOX K

Orienting Tasks and Recall: Hyde and Jenkins (1973)

Rationale
Hyde and Jenkins were interested in the effects of various orienting tasks on long-term memory. Accordingly, they made use of five different orienting tasks that appeared to vary in the amount of processing of meaning they required. They expected that those tasks requiring the processing of meaning would lead to better memory than those that did not. They also tested whether the commonsense view that intentional learning is superior to incidental learning is correct.

Method
A list of twenty-four words was presented auditorily at a rate of one word every three seconds. While the list was being presented, each subject performed one of the following orienting tasks:

1 Rating the words for pleasantness.
2 Estimating the frequency with which the words are used in the language.
3 Detecting 'e's and 'g's in the words.
4 Deciding the part of speech appropriate to each word (noun, verb, adjective, or 'some other' part of speech).
5 Making decisions as to whether or not the list of words fitted sentence frames ('it is the — '; 'it is — ').

These orienting tasks were performed in either an incidental learning condition (they did not expect to have to recall the list of words) or an intentional learning condition (they knew they would have to recall

---

the list). There were also control subjects who received intentional learning instructions but no orienting task. Each subject only performed one orienting task under one set of instructions. After the entire list of words had been presented, there was a test of free recall.

Results

The results are shown in Figure 2.8 and contain several features of interest. Hyde and Jenkins argued that rating pleasantness and rating frequency of usage were both orienting tasks that required semantic processing (i.e. analysis of meaning), whereas none of the other orienting tasks did. You may not agree with them, but we will reserve discussion of this point until later. Therefore, as Craik and Lockhart (1972) would predict, deep or semantic processing produced much better long-term memory than shallow or non-semantic processing.

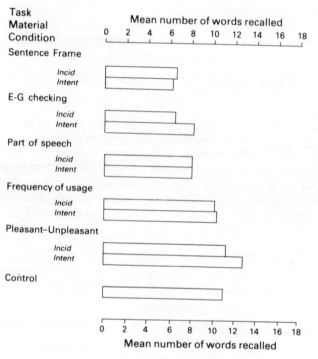

Figure 2.8 Free recall as a function of orienting task and learning instructions (adapted from Hyde and Jenkins, 1973)

Interpretation

You may find it surprising that there were negligible differences in free recall between intentional and incidental learners performing the same orienting task. Further evidence that simply intending to learn has little or no effect is suggested by the fact that intentional learners given no orienting task were no better than incidental learners given a semantic task. What do these findings mean? In line with the levels-of-processing theory, it seems that what is important in determining long-term memory is the nature of processing activities rather than the intention to learn *per se*.

Many other studies have replicated the patterns of results reported by Hyde and Jenkins (1973), and have thus supported the levels-of-processing theory. However, Craik and Lockhart (1972) put forward other theoretical notions that have fared less well. They distinguished between two types of processing or rehearsal: 'Type I processing, that is, repetition of analyses which have already been carried out, may be contrasted with Type II processing which involves deeper analysis of the stimulus. Only this second type of rehearsal should lead to improved memory performance' (p. 676). The most interesting notion is that there is a form of rehearsal (i.e. Type I processing) that does not enhance long-term memory.

There has been little disagreement with the notion that Type II or elaborative rehearsal improves long-term memory, but the proposal that Type I also known as *rote repetition* or *maintenance rehearsal* has no beneficial effect on long-term memory has met with much opposition. It turns out that maintenance rehearsal (e.g. the rote repetition of random digits) sometimes enhances long-term memory but at other times it does not. The kind of retention test is an important factor, in particular whether memory is tested by recall (when the items must be produced from memory) or by recognition (when list and non-list items are both presented, and the subject must decide which are from the list). For example, Glenberg, Smith, and Green (1977) discovered that the percentage of correct recognitions went up substantially from 65 to 74 as the time allowed for maintenance rehearsal increased from 2 to 18 seconds, but the same nine-fold increase in rehearsal time produced a negligible 1.5 per cent improvement in recall. It thus appears to be the case that recognition memory is more sensitive than recall to the effects of maintenance rehearsal.

Such findings clearly pose a problem for the levels-of-processing theory. However, since maintenance rehearsal typically improves memory much less than elaborative rehearsal, it may be worth preserving some form of distinction between different kinds of rehearsal. As teachers have long known, pupils remember their lessons much better if they work at understanding the underlying principles rather than simply learning by rote rehearsal. Perhaps we should replace the original sharp distinction between maintenance and elaborative rehearsal with a continuum of rehearsal activities ranging from mere rote rehearsal to highly elaborate memory strategies.

SAQ 12
How easy is it to decide whether an orienting task involves deep or shallow processing? Do you agree with Hyde and Jenkins?

Summary of Section 4.1

● According to the levels-of-processing theory, deep or semantic processing leads to better long-term memory than shallow or non-semantic processing.
● A distinction can be drawn between maintenance rehearsal (i.e. rote repetition of analyses already carried out) and elaborative rehearsal (i.e. processing which involves deeper analysis of the stimulus). Elaborative rehearsal is more beneficial than maintenance rehearsal in terms of enhancing long-term memory.
● Much of the experimental evidence supports the basic assumptions of levels-of-processing theory. It has been definitely established that processing activities at the time of learning can have a major impact on subsequent retention.

4.2 Elaboration and distinctiveness

While the original levels-of-processing theory was attractively simple, it always seemed unlikely that depth of processing is the only major factor in determining long-term memory. The original theory also suffered from a serious limitation that was not widely appreciated at the time: the theory is actually more of a description than an explanation. This can be seen quite clearly if we ask why it is that semantic processing usually leads to better memory than non-semantic processing. The answer provided by Craik and Lockhart (1972) is that depth of processing determines how well information is retained. Such an answer unfortunately fails to tell us *why* deep processing is so effective.

A number of theorists (e.g. Anderson and Reder, 1979) have attempted to resolve some of these problems by extending levels-of-processing theory to include *elaboration*. It seems indisputable that there is usually greater scope for elaborate or extensive processing at the semantic level than at other levels. For example, a word such as 'child' can be pronounced or spelled correctly in only one way, but may be richly processed in terms of its meaning (e.g. a young person; of immature behaviour and personality; one's own child; a friend's child; and so on).

The crucial assumption made by Anderson and Reder is that deep or semantic encodings tend to be more elaborate than shallow or non-semantic ones, and this is why more information is stored in memory after deep processing than after shallow processing. All that has to be assumed is that the more information that is stored about a stimulus or event, the easier it is subsequently to locate it in the memory system.

One of the earliest systematic investigations of elaboration was by Craik and Tulving (1975). They presented their subjects with a sentence containing a blank space and a separate word on each trial, and asked them to decide whether the word fitted sensibly into the blank space in the sentence. Some of the sentence frames were elaborate (e.g. *The great bird swooped down and carried off the struggling . . .*), followed by a word like 'HARE' or 'BOOK'. Others were simple and non-elaborate (e.g. *She cooked the . . .*).

After all of the sentences had been presented, there was an unexpected memory test in which the sentence frames were re-presented, and subjects attempted to recall the words that had been presented with them. In spite of the fact that the deep or semantic level of processing was involved throughout, recall was much higher for words accompanying elaborate sentence frames than for words presented with non-elaborate frames. Thus, elaboration of processing needs to be considered in addition to, or even instead of, processing depth.

So far we have seen that some theorists interested in the effects of processing at the time of acquisition on subsequent retention have emphasized the depth of processing, whereas others have focused on the amount of elaboration. Without wishing to make matters unnecessarily complex, it needs to be pointed out that other theorists (including myself) have argued that still other factors are important. Is it really true (as elaboration theorists often assume) that all that is important for long-term memory is the sheer number of elaborations? The notion that the precise nature of the elaborations that are formed is important was supported by Bransford, Franks, Morris and Stein (1979). They presented similes that were either multiply elaborated (e.g. *A mosquito is like a racoon because they both have heads, legs, jaws*) or minimally elaborated (e.g. *A mosquito is like a doctor because they both draw blood*). They then assessed recall by presenting the subject nouns in each sentence (e.g. 'mosquito') and asking for recall of the object nouns ('racoon' or 'doctor').

Elaboration theory predicts that simile recall should be better for the multiply elaborated similes (with three elements in common) than for the minimally elaborated ones (with only one element in common). In fact, the results obtained by Bransford *et al.* were diametrically opposed to the prediction. In other words, the sheer number of elaborations is not the crucial factor in affecting memory; rather, it is the case that precise and distinctive elaborations are more effective than imprecise and non-distinctive ones.

Another way of looking at this study is to argue that analogies like *A mosquito is like a doctor because they both draw blood* are well remembered because they 'stand out' in some way. Such findings have led various theorists (Eysenck, 1979; Jacoby and Craik, 1979) to argue that encodings that are *distinctive* or unique in some way are more likely to be remembered than encodings that are not distinctive. For example, distinctive events such as the first manned landing on the moon in July 1969 or the marriage of Prince Charles and Lady Diana are easily remembered by nearly everyone. However, what may be called the 'distinctiveness paradox' must be considered. While distinctive events are easy to *recognize* if someone mentions them, they tend to be infrequently *recalled*. When was the last time you thought about the first manned landing on the moon? The reason is that distinctive or unique encodings tend to be formed in the presence of very unusual events, and so the appropriate environmental stimuli for triggering recall of such encodings are rarely encountered. Part III discusses the retrieval environment in more detail.

TECHNIQUES BOX L

Distinctiveness and Memory: Eysenck (1979)

Rationale
In order to decide whether distinctiveness or depth was the important determinant of long-term memory, Eysenck (1979) attempted to produce memory traces that were non-semantic and thus shallow, but nevertheless distinctive or unique. Distinctiveness theory would predict that long-term memory should be good in this condition, whereas levels-of-processing theory predicts poor retention.

Method
96 nouns were presented from a pool of 240 nouns having irregular *grapheme–phoneme correspondence*. These are words that are not pronounced in conformity with normal pronunciation rules (e.g. 'glove' which would rhyme with 'cove' if it had regular grapheme–phoneme correspondence). Incidental learning was used, and subjects were asked to perform each of the following orienting tasks on one quarter of the words:

1 *Phonemic non-distinctive:* pronounce each word with its usual pronunciation ('glove' as in 'love').

2 *Phonemic distinctive:* pronounce each word as if it had regular grapheme–phoneme correspondence ('glove' as in 'cove').

3 *Semantic non-distinctive:* produce an adjective that is commonly used to modify each noun ('leather glove').

4 *Semantic distinctive:* produce an adjective that can be, but infrequently is, used to modify each noun ('oily glove').

The most important condition is the phonemic distinctive condition: it should produce encodings that are shallow, but distinctive or unique. The retention interval was 5 minutes, and was filled with an irrelevant non-verbal task. This was followed by free recall (i.e. recall in any order) or recognition (i.e. select the 96 words that had been presented from the entire pool of 240 words).

Results

	Words correct	
	Recognition	Recall
Phonemic non-distinctive	16.1	2.4
Phonemic distinctive	20.3	5.0
Semantic non-distinctive	20.8	6.4
Semantic distinctive	21.3	5.6

In recognition memory, phonemic distinctive encodings were recognized virtually as well as semantic encodings and much better than non-distinctive encodings. This suggests that distinctiveness can sometimes have more effect than depth of processing in determining long-term memory. However, the results were less clearcut with respect to recall. There was also not much of an effect due to semantic distinctiveness.

The distinctiveness approach has an immediate appeal. It seems reasonable to assume that some memory traces 'stand out' from other memory traces because they are different in the same way that a black cat in a green field is readily seen. However, it is often rather difficult to decide how distinctive an encoding actually is because there is no proper operational definition of distinctiveness. Distinctiveness depends, at least in part, on the context in which a particular stimulus is processed. Thus, in an example discussed by Eysenck (1984), the name 'Smith' if presented in the list 'Jones, Robinson, Williams, Baker, Smith, Robertson' would obviously not be distinctive, whereas it would stand out in the following list: 'Zzitz, Zysblat, Vangeersdaele, Vythelingum, Smith, Uwejeyah' (for which I am indebted to the London Telephone Directory). Distinctiveness would also vary from individual to individual, depending on their previous experiences.

Psychologists have disagreed as to which aspect of processing of inputs is of greatest importance in predicting recall. The major contenders are *depth of processing*, *elaboration of processing*, and *distinctiveness of processing*. Why has it proved so difficult to adjudicate between these three aspects of processing? A large part of the problem is that all three aspects tend to co-vary. Deep encodings are usually also elaborate and distinctive, whereas shallow encodings tend to be non-elaborate and non-distinctive. As a consequence, the three factors of depth, elaboration and distinctiveness are difficult to isolate from each other at the empirical level. However, in spite of these uncertainties, certain points have been established. Long-term memory is *not* determined solely by the depth or level of processing, because more elaborate or distinctive encodings are generally much better remembered than relatively non-elaborate or non-distinctive encodings. Perhaps the most reasonable conclusion is that all three factors contribute to long-term memory, with the relative importance of each factor remaining to be determined by future research.

Summary of Section 4.2

- In general, greater elaboration of processing leads to better long-term memory.
- There is also evidence that the distinctiveness or uniqueness of processing affects long-term memory, especially when a recognition test is used.
- It is difficult to distinguish empirically among the effects of depth, elaboration and distinctiveness.

4.3 Evaluation of levels of processing

The levels-of-processing approach has had a curiously chequered history. It was probably the most influential theoretical approach in the field of memory during much of the 1970s, but thereafter it rapidly fell from favour. It is probably only now that a balanced view is possible.

On the credit side, Craik and Lockhart (1972) were absolutely right to argue that perception, attention and memory should be regarded as interdependent. Once it is recognized that memory traces are formed as a result of perceptual and attentional processes, it becomes vital for memory research to focus on the nature of such processes. At this very general level, I would agree that the levels-of-processing approach has made a major contribution. You may feel that it is fairly obvious that memory depends on the specific processing activities performed at the time of learning but the fact remains that, prior to 1972, remarkably few experiments compared the effects on memory of different kinds of processing. The implicit assumption seems to have been that a particular stimulus will typically be processed in a very similar way by all subjects and on all occasions.

On the debit side, a pressing problem is the difficulty of determining what the level or depth of processing actually is in any particular case. The problem can be illustrated by returning to the study by Hyde and Jenkins (1973) that was discussed in Techniques Box K. They claimed that judging the frequency of a word requires some consideration of its meaning, whereas deciding the part of speech to which a word belongs does not. However, both of these claims can be (and have been) disputed. There is no way to resolve such disputes because there is no adequate measure of processing depth.

A further problem that is less obvious but just as serious can also be discussed with reference to the study of Hyde and Jenkins. They (in common with other researchers) used only a test of free recall to measure long-term memory. Strictly speaking, therefore, we can only use their data to conclude that deep encodings are better remembered than shallow encodings when recall is tested. It is not clear whether similar results would have been obtained if a different retention test had been used. This problem is discussed in Techniques Box M.

TECHNIQUES BOX M

Depth of Processing and Retrieval Conditions: Morris, Bransford and Franks (1977)

Rationale
Morris, Bransford and Franks (1977) argued that the effects of different processing activities on memory are often substantially affected by the nature of the test used to measure retention. More specifically, they proposed that stored information (whether deep or shallow) will be remembered only to the extent that it is of *relevance* to the test of memory that is used. As a consequence, deep or semantic information would be of little use if the memory test involved learning a list of words and later selecting words that rhymed with the stored list words, but shallow rhyme information would be of particular relevance with such a memory test.

Method
In the initial orienting task, the experimenter read aloud 32 sentences with one word missing from each. Each sentence was followed by the vocal presentation of the target word. The task was to respond positively or negatively as to the appropriateness of the target if inserted within the preceding sentence (half required a 'yes' response and the other half

97

a 'no' response). For half of the sentences the input orienting task was semantic, and for the other half there was a rhyme orienting task. That is, half required semantic processing of the target words (e.g. . . . *had a silver engine*), and the remainder required phonemic processing (e.g. *The . . . rhymes with legal*). All subjects heard all of the sentences.

Half of the subjects then received a standard recognition test in which the 32 original targets mixed with 32 distractors were presented and the subjects had to respond 'Yes' to the targets and 'No' to the distractors. The remaining subjects were given a rhyming recognition test. New words (not the original targets) were presented. Subjects had to respond 'Yes' to those new words that rhymed with the original targets and 'No' to those that did not.

Results
Recognition–memory performance for those words that had been associated with 'No' answers on the initial orienting task proved difficult to interpret. Performance for those words that had been associated with 'Yes' answers is shown in Figure 2.9.

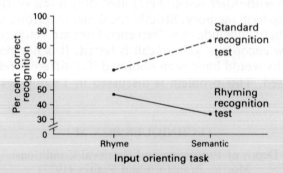

Figure 2.9 Recognition performance as a function of orienting task and retrieval conditions (Morris, Bransford and Franks, 1977)

The usual depth effect of deep processing leading to better retention than shallow processing was obtained with the standard recognition test. However, the fact that shallow processing led to significantly better recognition performance than deep processing with the rhyming recognition test provides an experimental disproof of levels-of-processing theory. In addition, the results demonstrate that the ways in which memory is tested must be considered when we are attempting to predict the consequences of some processing activity.

Interpretation
The findings support the notion that long-term memory is determined by the relevance of stored information to any given retention test. Rather than just considering processes occurring at input, we must consider both input processes and the way in which memory is tested.

The typical experimental approach of comparing the consequences of various orienting tasks is based upon the assumption that the subject's processing of a set of stimuli is determined exclusively by the particular orienting task set by the experimenter.

We can usually be confident that the specified task demands have been complied with by looking at the overt responses produced by each subject. However, there is an ever-present danger that the subject will engage in extraneous processing that is unrelated to the orienting task. Consider again the data of Hyde and Jenkins (1973), who discovered that subjects asked to check for the letters 'e' and 'g' in a word list were nevertheless able to recall an average of seven of the words in a subsequent retention test. It seems unlikely that 'proofreading' for two letters of the alphabet could have produced this level of recall. So in this case (and numerous others) some other processing must have occurred. However, this does not totally invalidate the experimental results — the fact that different orienting tasks lead to very different levels of retention indicates that the orienting tasks do exert a strong influence on processing activities. All that needs to be borne in mind is that such control is not absolute.

What does the future hold for levels-of-processing theory? I have recently argued at some length (Eysenck, 1984) that the original theory focused too narrowly on processing activities occurring at acquisition, virtually ignoring all other determinants of long-term memory. More specifically, I pointed out (1984, p. 114) that learning and memory are affected by at least four types of factors:

1 The nature of the task given to the subject.

2 The kind of stimulus materials presented to the subject.

3 The individual characteristics of the subjects (e.g. their idiosyncratic knowledge).

4 The nature of the retention test used to measure memory.

All of these factors are clearly of relevance in the teaching situation. Teachers rapidly discover that those children who already possess the most relevant knowlege tend to learn more quickly than those who cannot fit the new material into an appropriate context. The speed with which children learn is also obviously affected by the learning materials provided and by the way they are instructed to use that material. The notion that a child's apparent memory for previous lessons depends critically on the way that memory is tested is perhaps not always fully appreciated in the teaching situation. There is a tendency to argue that, if a child 'really knows' something, then the way in which memory is tested does not matter. But, as I am sure you will agree, you may not be able to recall material that you 'really know' in the type of retention test known as an exam.

In much of the research on levels of processing, there are several orienting tasks, but only one kind of stimulus material (usually words), one relatively homogeneous set of subjects, and one retention test. The most important single reason why such narrowness is inadequate is because there are often large interactions among the four factors described above. The effects of different kinds of processing on memory depend on the nature of the stimulus materials, the characteristics of the subjects, and the form of the retention test. For example, in the study by Morris *et al.* (1977) described in Techniques Box M, the usual superiority of deep over shallow encodings was obtained with one retention test, but exactly the opposite finding was obtained with a different retention test. The message is that the insights of levels-of-processing theory need to be incorporated into a broader theoretical framework in which more attention is given to the ways in which memories depend critically on other aspects of the learning and retrieval environments.

SAQ 13
Why can our findings be misleading if we focus only on the effects of processing activities on memory?

Summary of Section 4.3

- It is very difficult to establish the depth of processing associated with a particular orienting task.
- The effects of different processing activities on long-term memory depend on the precise form of the memory test: stored information must be relevant to the particular memory test used.
- Memory is affected by processing activities at the time of learning, but it is also affected by the stimulus materials, individual differences, and the type of memory test.

5 *Levels-of-processing theory and working memory: some conclusions*

Now that we have discussed the working memory model and levels-of-processing theory, it is worthwhile to consider how they relate to each other. At a general level, both theories emphasize the notion that there are several different active processing strategies that can be applied to incoming stimulus information. Perhaps both theories would also agree that attentional processes provide much of this flexibility of processing. Of course, Craik and Lockhart (1972) were interested in the issue of how these various processing activities affect long-term memory, whereas Baddeley and Hitch (1974) investigated the role of working memory in problem solving, reading and so on.

Given that the various processing activities studied by Craik and Lockhart presumably involve the resources of working memory, it would seem that there is scope for a fruitful dialogue between the two approaches. For example, it is tempting to argue that maintenance rehearsal and the articulatory loop have much in common. Unfortunately, these two lines of research have tended to be carried out in isolation, each developing its own experimental methods.

In the future, exciting developments may occur if there is some amalgamation of ideas from the two theoretical approaches. For example, consider the simple distinction between deep and shallow processing put forward by Craik and Lockhart (1972).

The relationship between the levels-of-processing and working memory approaches could be explored in the typical levels-of-processing paradigm in which different subjects are given different orienting tasks to perform. The consequences for long-term memory of performing some additional task at the same time as carrying out an orienting task could be of interest. For example, articulatory suppression might reduce memory when an orienting task requiring phonemic coding was used, but not when an adjective task was used. This would indicate that the articulatory loop is involved in the phonemic task but not in the more semantic adjective task. In this way, the involvement of the various components of working memory in the performance of different learning processes could be assessed.

During the course of this Part, I have identified a number of uncertainties that will require further consideration in the future. For example, very little is known about the central executive, and the precise relationship between the acoustic store and the articulatory loop remains to be worked out. As was discussed in the previous section, there are also various issues concerning the extent to which the levels-of-processing and working memory formulations can be combined and integrated.

A major limitation of both the working memory model and levels-of-processing is that they have very little to say about the changes in strategy that occur over time as a result of practice. For example, we all know that driving a car is extraordinarily demanding for a learner driver, but relatively effortless for an experienced one. In similar fashion, expert mathematicians might be able to perform effortlessly mental calculations that would be almost impossible for other people to do. Of course, this change can be described in terms of a reduction in the use of the attentional resources of the central executive with practice, but this does not even begin to explain what has happened.

In this connection, a useful distinction (introduced in Part I, Section 5.1) has been suggested between attentional processing, which requires conscious control, and automatic processing (Shiffrin and Schneider, 1977). There has been a certain amount of disagreement about the defining criteria for automatic processing, but the main criteria adopted include occurring without awareness, highly efficient, without capacity limitations, difficult to modify, and involuntary (LaBerge, 1981). It appears that well-learned complex tasks can sometimes become automatic and can be performed without making any use of the resources of working memory. Of course, substantial amounts of practice are typically needed to achieve automaticity, and automaticity only develops when task demands are relatively invariant. However, there are grounds for arguing that the importance of conscious attention has been exaggerated. At the very least, we need to know more about why it is that the involvement of working memory in the performance of a task can be reduced substantially with extended practice.

Finally, it is likely that the working memory system can be used even more flexibly than has generally been assumed. In particular, it is unwise to assume that the components of working memory used in the performance of a given task are always the same. For example, it has often been assumed that memory span for digits involves the articulatory loop, and, as predicted, articulatory suppression reduces digit span. Suppose we gave people massive practice at the digit-span task under articulatory suppression conditions. Is it not likely that they would develop some alternative strategy for performing the digit-span task without using the articulatory loop? They might develop a strategy based on using their fingers to store some of the digits, like the 'typing' strategies described by Reisberg *et al*. (1984) (described in Section 3.4).

There is a saying that good research raises more questions than it answers, and that is certainly applicable to the work carried out with the levels-of-processing and working models.

Further reading

Baddeley, A. D. (1982) 'Domains of recollection', *Psychological Review, 89*, 708–729, and in A. Aitkenhead and J. Slack (eds) (1985) *Issues in Cognitive Modeling*, Erlbaum. Provides a critical evaluation of levels of processing in comparison with other theories.
Eysenck, M. W. (1984) *A Handbook of Cognitive Psychology*, London, Erlbaum (especially Chapters 4 and 5). Covers some of the same ground as this Part, but in greater detail.

PART III
Encoding and Retrieval in Recognition and Recall

Martin Le Voi

Contents

1   *Introduction*

> Suppose I am silent for a moment, and then say, in commanding accents: 'Remember! Remember!' Does your faculty of memory obey the order and reproduce any definite image from your past? Certainly not. It stands staring into vacancy, and asking, 'What kind of a thing do you wish me to remember?' It needs, in short, a *cue*. (William James, 1899, pp. 117–8)

This early quotation from an Old Master of Psychology illustrates the central importance of retrieval cues for the successful operation of memory. If we were simply to 'turn on' our memory system in response to William James' command to 'Remember', but give the system no direction or guidance about what to remember, our mind would fill with all kinds of random, unrelated images, thoughts and concepts, with perhaps even less meaning than the average dream.

Our memory system contains a vast amount of stored experience. Re-read Part I, pp. 51–2. Those studies of everyday memory showed that there were huge quantities of knowledge available, but to get at them required considerable effort by the rememberer. To release the stored knowledge on demand in a meaningful and controlled way, the memory system has to be interrogated, using carefully designed and selected *retrieval cues*, which both permit access to the area of memory where the wanted information is found, and prevent unwanted access to irrelevant information.

In Part I, pp. 51–2, studies of everyday memory were described in which protocols were taken from the human subjects to track the way the cues were derived, selected and used. The process was described as 'generating a context within which to search', 'recreating the contexts in which the items were originally embedded' and 'matching a retrieved item against the specification'. These phrases all refer to the creation, selection, refinement and use of retrieval cues. This experimental situation is called *free recall*, since the subject is free to recall any items (in that case names of colleagues) and create and use helpful cues in any way he or she wishes. But studying the operations of memory in such an open-ended way, while often illuminating, makes it difficult to discover exactly how the retrieval cues interrogate the memory system, or what it is that the memory system has stored in it. The problem is that everyone has completely different memories of the past; there is no control of the way the cues are created and selected, and indeed there may well be considerable differences between subjects in the way cues are created and used to interrogate memory.

For these reasons and others, many psychologists turned to the laboratory to study controlled experiments using *cued recall*. There is no clear-cut boundary between 'free' recall and 'cued' recall, because as we have seen above, even free recall does not proceed without any cues at all. However, the aim of experiments in cued recall is to attempt to cut out all the subjects' personal strategies for generating their own cues by providing them with a set of direct, strongly focused cues, which are designed to be rather better than those they could generate for themselves. The power of the technique is also increased by restricting the to-be-remembered items (*target stimuli*) to lists of words which are presented to the subject in an orderly way, so as to avoid the problem of different subjects having very different memories.

For example, this could be achieved by presenting the word CHAIR as part of a list of words to be remembered, and then providing (at the time of recall) the word *table* as a cue for recall of CHAIR. The cue is said to be *associated* with the target word, and a different *associate cue* would be provided for each target word in the list. Certainly these cued recall experiments do provide higher levels of list recall than subjects can achieve just by being asked to free recall the list of words without any specific cues being supplied (e.g. Thomson and Tulving, 1970), so it appears reasonable to assume that the cues are indeed better than the ones that the subjects could generate for themselves.

These laboratory studies of cued recall have attempted to discover the way in which cues provided by the experimenter (rather than created by the subject) operate to retrieve information from the memory system, and also to discover how memories for lists of items such as words, faces, etc. are stored in the memory system.

The latter question revolves around the problem of what is *encoded* into our memory system. Part II described an approach (*levels of processing*) which considered that the manner of encoding, more precisely the *depth of encoding*, was heavily responsible for the efficiency of storage of information in memory.

The main aim of that approach was to determine the way that *encoding* operations affect stored information. You saw (Part II, Section 4) that there were three possible aspects of encoding which could be important: depth, elaboration and distinctiveness of processing. But it was also shown (p. 91) that the conclusions drawn were heavily dependent on the nature of the retention test used. Very different results were obtained when retention was tested using different types of cues. It is vital, therefore, to build up an understanding of how retrieval cues work and how different cues produce different results. In this way, by combining the insights about encoding operations provided by the levels-of-processing model with discoveries about retrieval cues, we can develop the broader conceptualization called for at the end of Part II.

It's worth refreshing your understanding of the distinction of semantic memory and episodic memory. The semantic memory system contains all the information you know about the world in general, things like your language, where you live, what things are edible and what are poisonous, etc. As you read these words, it is your semantic memory system which helps to identify each word and supplies its meaning. The episodic memory system is responsible for recording (more or less) discrete time-based events or *episodes*, such as what you had to eat last night, the things that happened to you on holiday, the *events* of the Falklands war, such as the sinking of HMS Coventry, and so on. The experiments we shall use are almost exclusively laboratory-based, generally using individual words or word pairs as the *events* which are assumed to be stored as separate *episodes* in the memory system. In short, we are looking at laboratory studies of episodic memory. Part I concentrated on naturally occurring episodes in peoples' lives to provide the everyday memories which were the object of study; in the laboratory studies we shall be looking at in Part III, the episodes are specially created by presenting certain stimuli in particular, novel spatio-temporal contexts (see Part I, p. 46), which then form the episodic memories which are the object of study.

2   *Memory representation and processes*

Many theories of memory have used the idea that *memory traces* are stored in the memory system. These memory traces form the basic unit of representation in theories of episodic memory.

In episodic memory, the memory trace is considered to be a simple structure, often corresponding to a collection of information gathered from a single event. Any theory of memory needs to answer these basic questions:

1 How is the trace formed?
2 How is it stored?
3 How is it later retrieved?

Such questions are often conveniently summarized in *information processing models* like Figure 3.1.

In this model there are two vital processing stages.

1 In the *encoding process*, the physical characteristics of the stimulus (word, face etc.) are processed and *encoded* as a memory trace. Some of these processes correspond to the simple processing done by the perceptual systems in order to identify or categorize the input

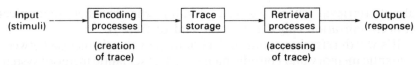

Figure 3.1   Stages of information processing

stimulus. Further processing may require a contribution from the semantic memory system, involving *elaborative processing*; the latter may result in encoding complex and elaborate memory traces containing information only loosely related to the original stimulus. Technically, researchers talk about information being 'encoded on the trace'.

2 In the *retrieval process* the memory trace is retrieved by operations designed first to access the correct memory trace, and then to derive useful information from it. These operations can also vary in complexity. Sometimes a cue may elicit the memory trace directly using simple matching strategies (direct access); at other times complicated search procedures are used, which attempt to narrow down the area of memory in various ways until all that is left is the required trace. This type of search often uses sophisticated generation and comparison procedures. One example of this is the attempt of the subject in the Williams and Hollan (1982) experiment to recall the names of classmates (see Part I, p. 52).

The greatest difficulty in all this, however, lies in identifying exactly what process underlies performance. There is no way we can plug into someone's brain and find out exactly what memory traces are lying there or what these memory traces have encoded on them. They are *unobservable*. And the encoding (input) and retrieval (output) operations are equally unobservable. Instead, they have to be inferred from the results of experimentation.

But where should we start? Is it possible to make deductions about one process without making assumptions about others? We will look closely at two attempts to model the processes involved in memory for specific events or episodes.

3   Encoding specificity

The first attempt we shall look at was championed by Endel Tulving at the end of the 1960s. He created the *Encoding Specificity Principle* which forms the basic theoretical assumption behind his theorizing.

The theory seeks to explain the operation of retrieving memory traces given certain cues. The Encoding Specificity Principle states that:

the cue will succeed at retrieving a memory trace if, *and only if*, the information contained by that cue is encoded on the memory trace.

It is called the Encoding Specificity Principle (usually abbreviated to ESP) because it assumes that the information *specific* to a cue must be *encoded* as part of the memory trace in order for the cue to work. This means that a memory trace is created which links together information about the cue with information about the target. As this forms the central axiom of Tulving's theory, this assumption of *encoding specificity* is known as a *principle*.

As an example, recall of the word CHAIR by means of the cue *table* could only succeed if the two words had been encoded as part of the same memory trace. So a memory trace is laid down in the episodic memory system which has encoded on it both information about CHAIR (the target) and *table* (the cue). When *table* is provided as a cue in a recall test, the correct memory trace is retrieved by a *direct match* to the trace (the information about *table* encoded on the trace and on the cue match up) and the target information (in this case the word CHAIR) is read off. This operation of direct matching of cues to traces is known as *direct access* retrieval. The corollary is that if cue information has not been encoded on the stored memory trace, then that information *cannot* successfully act as a retrieval cue.

3.1   Reduction method

How does Tulving use this principle to analyse memory? One major use is in the *reduction method* of analysing memory by cueing. It is very important that you complete the following activity (although your level of performance is not critical) since the concepts and methodology illustrated by it are directly relevant to everything in this Part.

Activity 1
Read through the following list of words, perhaps three or four times, but don't spend more than a minute overall. Then turn to page 148 to complete the activity. Don't waste time trying to memorize the list perfectly, you will spoil the demonstration if you do, and there are no prizes. In this activity, you should treat each word as an *individual* word, and not group them into pairs or triples. A 'real' experiment would present the words one at a time, but that is not possible here.

LAMB DAY FLOWER COAT BALL COLD PEACH BLUE SWEET SHORT

Turn to page 148 to complete the activity.

The point of this Activity is that there were *two* different forms of cues. The first type is a *rhyme cue*, so that the cue to help you remember the word BALL is *wall*. The second type of cue is an *associate cue*, so the cue for the word BALL is *tennis*, and the cue for COLD is *hot*. Almost certainly, there are some words you could remember to both types of cues, some to only one cue but not the other, and some words you could not remember to either cue. Note that the words were presented singly and, most importantly, the cues are words which were never presented in the learning phase of the experiment.

The initial aim of experiments like these is to create tables of results which reveal how well the different cues do, and the results are expressed in simple tables like you prepared at the end of the activity.

TECHNIQUES BOX N

Reduction Method

Rationale

The reduction method is a technique for measuring the relative *efficacy* of different types of cues.

Method

Subjects are presented with a list of stimulus items. These items can be of any form, such as words, pictures or faces. The critical point is that the items are presented singly, so that each may be assumed to represent one event which is encoded as a single episode in the memory system. After presentation of the list, there may be an intervening task designed to produce interference or to prevent rehearsal. Finally, memory for the stimulus items is tested by cueing with two or more cues for each item. These cues can be of any type, but are of at least two or more classes (such as rhyme and associate), so that each item is cued once by each class of cue. For any given word, one group of subjects will have one order of cueing (e.g. rhyme cue followed by associate cue) and the other group of subjects will have another order of cueing (e.g. associate cue followed by rhyme cue). However, each individual subject will have some of the items cued in one order of cueing, and others in another order.

Example: If the target words LAMB FLOWER PEACH BALL were presented one at a time as a list to be remembered, one group of subjects would have a test series like this:

Tram	(rhyme cue for LAMB)
Bloom	(associate cue for FLOWER)
Fruit	(associate cue for PEACH)
Wall	(rhyme cue for BALL)
Sheep	(associate cue for LAMB)
Power	(rhyme cue for FLOWER)
Teach	(rhyme cue for PEACH)
Tennis	(associate cue for BALL)

while another group would have a test series like this:

Sheep	(associate cue for LAMB)
Power	(rhyme cue for FLOWER)
Teach	(rhyme cue for PEACH)
Tennis	(associate cue for BALL)
Tram	(rhyme cue for LAMB)
Bloom	(associate cue for FLOWER)
Fruit	(associate cue for PEACH)
Wall	(rhyme cue for BALL)

In the series of tests the classes of cues occur apparently randomly, with associate cues and rhyme cues mixed together. Obviously, the two cues for the same words are separated so that there is no direct interference of one cue on another. Indeed, the tests are usually presented in such a way as to prevent the subjects from seeing previous responses.

Results

In the scoring, the number of items which are never recalled, and the number of items recalled to one class of cue after failure of the other class of cue, are entered into a table such as the one below, just like the final table which you completed in Activity 1. This is an example of a *2×2 table*, which has four individual (numbered) *cells*.

Table **3.1**   Summary table of results of the reduction method

		Rhyme cue	
		Success	Failure
Associate cue	Success	1	2 Recall to associate cue after failure of rhyme cue
	Failure	3 Recall to rhyme cue after failure of associate cue	4 Complete recall failure

The empty box 1 represents potential recall to both cues. Since the total of all four cells in the table must add up to the number of subject-item responses in the experiment it can easily be calculated. Usually, all the numbers are converted to percentages of the total recall so that the total sum of all four boxes is 100%. The calculation of this 2×2 table marks the end of the reduction method.

So what do these numbers represent? Tulving, by invoking the Encoding Specificity Principle (ESP), claims that the success or failure of each cue depends directly on whether information about that cue was encoded on the memory trace. If you remember, the ESP states that a cue can *only* succeed if information about that cue was encoded on the memory trace at the time it was created, i.e. when you first saw the item. If no information was encoded, the cue *must* fail. And it is usually accepted, for simplicity, that if information was encoded on the trace, the cue will always succeed. As a result, a successful cue reveals that the memory trace has that information on it, while a failed cue implies that information about that cue is not on the memory trace. Therefore, Tulving claims that the results of the reduction method, given by the four cells of the summary table, tell us the proportion of episodic memory traces which have information about both cues encoded on them (Cell 1), the proportion of traces that have associate cue but no rhyme cue information on them (Cell 2), the proportion of traces which have rhyme cue but no associate cue information on them (Cell 3), and the proportion of traces which have no information about either cue encoded on them (Cell 4).

3.2   Axioms, principles and circularity

Now you might think that this interpretation is rather *circular*: traces can only be retrieved if a cue was encoded on them, but the only way we can find out if the cue was encoded on the trace is by seeing if the cue produces retrieval! The theory is indeed circular, in fact it has to be, since the encoding or retrieval operations are intrinsically unobservable. Hence there can be no independent evidence that can reveal whether a cue has been encoded other than the fact that the cue supports recall. For instance, when you read the word BALL in Activity 1, you may have felt that there was no sense in which you encoded the word *tennis* along with it. But if the word *tennis* did succeed in retrieving the word BALL in the recall test, Tulving's theory maintains that *tennis* must have been *spontaneously encoded* along with BALL when you read the word and created a memory trace for that episode. There is no way of proving that this is not the case. It is not possible to *falsify* the Encoding Specificity Principle (ESP), because it does not allow a situation in which something can be retrieved by a cue which was *not* encoded. If a cue works (i.e. *supports recall*), by definition it must have been encoded. The idea of encoding specificity is therefore *unfalsifiable*, which is why the idea is known as a 'principle', rather than a hypothesis (hypotheses are supposed to be *falsifiable* by experimental test). Tulving's solution, to give us an unfalsifiable *axiom* or principle in the shape of the ESP, with a circular definition, acts as a basic axiom which allows us to use the reduction method to test theories about other memory phenomena.

This is similar to the way that Isaac Newton's laws of motion provided unfalsifiable axioms, in a circular model, which provided the base from which he could start theorizing about other phenomena, e.g. gravity. Newton's laws state that a body travels in a straight line unless a force acts upon it. A force is defined as something which causes a body to deviate from a straight line! This obvious circularity is powerful since it allowed Newton to theorize about gravity, which is the force that made the legendary apple fall on his head.

3.3   The structure of memory traces

Let us see how the ESP is used with the reduction method to calculate the probabilities that specific cue information is encoded on episodic memory traces. If both cues succeed in retrieving an item, it is assumed that a memory trace exists with both Associate and Rhyme cue information; this situation is usually represented by the abbreviation AR. If the rhyme cue succeeds but the associate cue fails, this is taken to mean that the trace has encoded rhyme cue information but not associate cue information, represented as R. A successful associate cue and a failed rhyme cue implies a trace with only associate cue information, represented as A. Finally, if neither cue succeeds, the trace is said to be empty or 'null'. So the experimental results in such an experiment imply that the following information is encoded on the memory trace.

Table 3.2 Memory trace structures identified by the ESP

| | | Rhyme cue | |
		Success	Failure
Associate cue	Success	AR	A
	Failure	R	null

Each cell in the table corresponds to a particular configuration which defines the *structure of the memory trace*. This means that there is a very simple correspondence between the table of results in the reduction method and the theoretical structure of the memory trace. The existence of four types of memory traces (AR, A, R and null) with varying combinations of cue information is the result of accepting the axiomatic ESP, and thus depends on this theory. It so happens that the probability of formation of each of these four memory trace structures is provided *directly* from the results of the reduction method. The value of A, for example, is obtained directly from the table of results of the reduction method (i.e. the number in Cell 2 in the summary Table 3.1). For example, look at the following summary table of results which we might have obtained from an experiment like Activity 1:

Table 3.3 Example of results from a reduction method experiment

		Rhyme cue	
		Success	Failure
Associate cue	Success	12%	18%
	Failure	8%	62%

This set of results would have been calculated using the reduction method, just as you did in Activity 1. As simple results of the experiment, they are not very interesting. The ESP, however, allows us to *interpret* each value and give it a meaning. Thus, in the conditions under which this experiment occurred we conclude that on 12% of occasions, a memory trace was laid down with the structure AR (i.e. the memory trace was encoded with both associate and rhyme information). Similarly, 18% of the memory traces had Associate cue information only (structure A), 8% had Rhyme cue information only (structure R) and 62% were null (i.e. neither A nor R information had been encoded). This *interpretation* is often also summarized as in Table 3.4.

Table 3.4

Type of trace structure	Probability of occurrence
AR	12%
A	18%
R	8%
null	62%

SAQ 14
Given the results from the reduction method in Table 3.5, interpret the results as occurrences of trace types and fill in the blanks in Table 3.6.

Table 3.5

| | | Rhyme cue | |
		Success	Failure
Associate cue	Success	70%	10%
	Failure	15%	5%

Table 3.6

Type of trace structure	Probability of occurrence
AR	
A	
R	
null	

One thing it is important to remember about the reduction method is that it takes into account the *order of cueing*. Half of the words were cued with the associate cue first, and the other half were cued with the rhyme cue first. Now it is generally agreed (and can be shown empirically) that there is a problem in these experiments if recall has succeeded on the first cue. This is because that success itself makes the second cue more likely to succeed — because, if you like, the word is still fresh in your mind after successfully remembering it, and is therefore more easily available for the following cue.

However, if the first cue fails, it is not considered that there is any effect on the second cue. In this situation, since recall has failed, there is no recalled word to remain 'fresh in your mind'. So the reduction method deliberately ignores performance on the second cue if the first cue was successful, but does use the results of the second cue if the first cue failed. As a result the cell for the case where both cues succeed cannot be calculated from the raw data, because obviously if both cues succeed, then no matter which order the cues came in, the second cue must have been preceded by a successful cue. However, with a bit of arithmetic (such as you performed in Activity 1), it is possible to reconstruct a set of results which are not biased by success in the first test, and these are the values produced by the reduction method to represent the cells in the overall table. These values are then interpreted by the ESP to give the trace structure, as we saw in the above example.

SAQ 15
Table 3.7 contains results from a reduction method experiment which used two orders of cueing, using rhyme and associate cues. Calculate the final summary table for the reduction method, using the same method step by step that you used in Activity 1. Enter your results in Table 3.8. (Because these numbers are already percentages, you only need to do the last stage of the calculation as set out in Activity 1.)

Start by looking for the two cases where the first cue failed but the second cue succeeded.

Table 3.7

		Associate cue first					Rhyme cue first	
		Rhyme cue					Rhyme cue	
		Success	Failure				Success	Failure
Associate cue	Success	31%	20%		Associate cue	Success	22%	16%
	Failure	14%	35%			Failure	17%	45%

Table 3.8

		Rhyme cue	
		Success	Failure
Associate cue	Success	1	2
	Failure	3	4

This then gives a very simple account of the way the memory trace structure underlying performance can be examined using the reduction method in this kind of experiment. If the encoding of the word includes information about a rhyme cue on it, then the memory trace will support recall to rhyme cues, and ditto for any other type of cue we may care to try out in these experiments. Similarly, the retrieval process is very simple, involving comparison of the cue presented at recall with cue information existing on the memory traces. If a match is found, the word is recalled; if not, it is assumed that the cue had not been encoded on the trace.

Summary of Sections 2 and 3

- Memory traces and processes are intrinsically unobservable.
- The Encoding Specificity Principle (ESP) is an attempt to define the conditions under which retrieval occurs. It states that 'the cue will succeed at retrieving a memory trace if, and only if, the information contained by that cue is encoded on the memory trace'.
- The reduction method uses retrieval cues to provide unbiased estimates of the probabilities of recall to each cue.
- According to the ESP, cues retrieve memory traces by *direct access*; the information provided by the cue is directly matched to the memory trace to produce recall.
- The ESP allows interpretation of the results of the reduction method as representing the occurrence of different types of memory trace structures, which in turn reveal the way memory traces have been *encoded* in memory.

4   Retrieval processes

We should now ask whether the ESP is a plausible account of memory. In Activity 1 the cues used in recall were not presented along with the target item. The subject didn't see the cues until they were given as cues in the recall tests. So how did the subject 'know' that she should be encoding the specific cues *tennis* and/or *wall* with the word BALL on a memory trace? Of course, subjects have no idea what cues will be used in the recall test, so they must encode all sorts of additional cue information, only some of which will happen to be useful for recall. For example, when encoding the word BALL, according to the ESP, several associate words, e.g. round, cricket (as well as tennis), may have been encoded on the memory trace although they were not used as cues. If this were not so, it would be most unlikely that a specific cue could succeed as often as it does. However, it seems implausible that we should encode such a large amount of seemingly redundant information about a word every time that we see it just in case it may come in useful later, when we want to remember it.

Another possible approach to these experimental results is to treat retrieval as a very much more *active* process than the rather passive mechanism of direct access retrieval (the comparison of cues with traces until a match is found). In particular, recall may involve active use

117

of an associate cue to create or *generate* alternative words until one is found which is *recognized* as being from the original list. This is a quite different retrieval system from direct access recall. This retrieval system is indirect because it involves the generation of candidates for recall which are then tested by means of a recognition judgment. It is a *generate–recognize model*.

Assuming that an item has been encoded in episodic memory, in this model all the exploitation of the cues occurs at retrieval. For instance, the associate cue *table* is used to generate associates to it (e.g. desk, kitchen) and if the generated associates include among them the target word CHAIR then it can be recognized as such.

Table 3.9   A comparison of the ESP model and the retrieval process model

	ESP	Retrieval process
Encoding	Elaborated copy of target item	Simple copy of target item
Retrieval	Direct access	Generate–recognize
	Cue is compared directly with traces until a match is found	Cue generates a set of candidates which are then compared with memory in a recognition judgment

It is important to realize how radically different the generate–recognize way of recalling items is to the direct access recall postulated by the ESP. Tulving explicitly rejects the idea that active processes operate indirectly at retrieval and insists that the cue will only work if the correct encoding has been laid down in the episodic memory system. So where does this different approach leave the reduction method? The method itself is unaffected, because it is a technique for calculating unbiased estimates of retrieval cue efficacy, and it does not matter, as far as the reduction method is concerned, exactly how the cue operates. The summary table produced by the reduction method is still valid. What changes is the *interpretation* of those results.

In this new interpretation, the following assumptions are made:
1 Memory traces do not have elaborate structures, containing all kinds of extra information encoded on them. Indeed, the memory trace may consist of no more than a simple copy of the original item.
2 The target item may not have been encoded in memory at all.
3 The recall search from a particular type of cue has a given chance of success or failure.

These assumptions allow us to interpret the results of the reduction method in a different way.

4.1   Retrieval-process interpretation of the reduction method

The aim of this analysis is to show that any set of results from an experiment which uses the reduction method can be interpreted in terms of retrieval searches, and that we can calculate the probabilities of successful search given certain types of cues from those results, just as we can calculate the probabilities of the four trace types which exist according to the ESP. We will then ask how we can decide which theoretical approach should be considered the most appropriate. This analysis was first proposed by Le Voi, Ayton, Jonckheere, McClelland and Rawles (1983).

We have to calculate three probabilities. The first is the probability that an item (*on its own*) has been encoded (i.e. a memory trace has been created), which we can represent as T_r. Since all probabilities vary between zero and 100%, and since the alternative to a trace existing is the situation where the trace does *not*, we can work out the probability that there is no trace of an item as $100\% - T_r$. We also want to calculate the chance of success of generating a target item at retrieval from an associate cue, which we can represent by A_s. In other words, given an associate cue like *tennis*, a retrieval search is started which generates associates to the word *tennis*, and this process has a certain chance of including the target memory trace BALL. This probability of successful generation (or search) is written as A_s. The probability of failure of this search is therefore $100\% - A_s$. Finally the chance of successfully generating the target from a rhyme cue is represented as R_s, and the probability of its failure as $100\% - R_s$.

Now we can see how the various cells in the reduction method table can be derived. Let's start with the cell where both cues individually succeed at retrieving the item. For the cues to succeed, there must have been a memory trace of the item in the memory system, so the memory trace must have existed (with probability T_r). Also, both cues must have successfully generated the target for recall to occur from each one, the associate cue succeeding with probability A_s and the rhyme cue succeeding with probability R_s. So we can see that, when list words are recalled to both of the cues, we require a combination of

1 A memory trace of the item existing (T_r)
   AND
2 The associate cue retrieval search succeeding (A_s)
   AND
3 The rhyme cue retrieval search succeeding (R_s)

When probabilities are combined by AND in this way, the correct arithmetic step to perform is multiplication. So the results of this cell are represented by the product of the three probabilities:

$$T_r \times R_s \times A_s$$

This is the interpretation of Cell 1 in the reduction method summary table (Table 3.1).

The derivation of the other cells follows naturally. When the associate cue succeeds and the rhyme cue fails, we again know that a memory trace of the item must have existed (because otherwise no cue could succeed). So now the combination of chances is that a memory trace exists (T_r) AND the associate cue retrieval succeeds (A_s) AND the rhyme cue retrieval *fails* $(100\% - R_s)$. Again, these probabilities are multiplied together to reflect the AND combination:

$$T_r \times (100\% - R_s) \times A_s$$

This is the interpretation of Cell 2 in the reduction method summary table.

Similarly, when the rhyme cue succeeds and the associate cue fails we know that a memory trace exists AND the rhyme cue retrieval succeeds AND the associate cue retrieval fails, which is represented thus:

$$T_r \times R_s \times (100\% - A_s)$$

This is the interpretation of Cell 3 in the reduction method summary table.

Finally, Cell 4 results when both cues individually fail. So this could have resulted from a situation where the memory trace of an item exists AND both the associate cue retrieval fails AND the rhyme cue retrieval fails:

$$T_r \times (100\% - R_s) \times (100\% - A_s)$$

But recall also fails if there was no memory trace of an item at all. In this situation, it doesn't make any difference whether the retrieval searches would have succeeded or not, because there was no memory trace anyway. So in fact complete failure to recall arises EITHER as a result of the above situation (where both retrieval searches fail to access an existing memory trace) OR from the situation where there is no memory trace $(100\% - T_r)$. When probabilities are combined by OR, the correct arithmetic to do is addition, so we can write this cell as:

$$T_r \times (100\% - R_s) \times (100\% - A_s) + (100\% - T_r)$$

Table 3.10 shows the complete table. It is the retrieval process equivalent of Table 3.2 for the ESP.

The upshot of this is that when an experiment which uses the reduction method has been done to give a 2×2 table of results, a little arithmetic can provide the values of the various individual probabilities, T_r, A_s and R_s. This means we can calculate the chances of success of the retrieval searches as directed from each of the two cues, and the

Table 3.10   Retrieval process analysis of reduction method summary table.

| | | Rhyme cue | |
		Success	Failure
Associate cue	Success	**1** $T_r \times R_s \times A_s$	**2** $T_r \times (100\% - R_s \times A_s$
	Failure	**3** $T_r \times R_s \times (100\% - A_s)$	**4** $T_r \times (100\% - R_s)$ $\times (100\% - A_s)$ $+ (100\% - T_r)$

probability that a memory trace of an item exists, from the summary table of results of the reduction method.

As an example, let's have another look at the set of results we used to demonstrate the ESP interpretation of the reduction method.

Table 3.11

| | | Rhyme cue | |
		Success	Failure
Associate cue	Success	12%	18%
	Failure	8%	62%

These numbers have been calculated by following the reduction method. As we showed above, the ESP interpretation is that these numbers directly reflect the existence of various memory trace structures, with 12% being AR traces, 18% being A traces, 8% being R traces and 62% being null. However, the retrieval process model interpretation is that the results reflect the efficiency of retrieval searches, and we can calculate (from equations which are given in the appendix on p. 152) that the generation of words from the rhyme cue has a 40% chance of success of finding the target, the generation of words from the associate cue has a 60% chance of success, while the chance of a memory trace being stored (T_r) is 50%. This can also be summarized in a table:

Table 3.12

T_r	50%
R_s	40%
A_s	60%

In case you are concerned that A_s is found to be higher than T_r, you must remember that A_s is not the probability that recall will succeed from an associate cue. It is only the chance that the retrieval search will successfully generate the target item as a candidate. If, however, the target item was never encoded, this effort is wasted and cannot succeed. Recall of a word from an associate cue depends on *both* a memory trace existing *and* the retrieval search successfully generating a candidate.

This model produces the same numbers as you see in the 2×2 summary table (Table 3.11). You can verify for yourself that, for instance, $T_r \times A_s \times R_s = 50\% \times 40\% \times 60\% = 12\%$, the figure for both cues succeeding.

SAQ 16
Check the values in the other three cells by doing the calculations for yourself. In other words, find the values of the three remaining cells in the reduction method summary table, given $R_s = 40\%$, $A_s = 60\%$ and $T_r = 50\%$.

This means that the model based on retrieval processes can produce an explanation of the results of this experiment which is numerically every bit as good as the ESP model. We have to think of other ways of choosing which model is best.

4.2 Encoding specificity or retrieval processes?

So there are at least two ways of interpreting the results of experiments which use the reduction method. The first, derived from the Encoding Specificity Principle, postulates the encoding of episodic memory traces with an elaborate structure, consisting of the target word plus various associates or attributes which can support recall when used as cues. The experimental data are used to deduce the relative occurrence of various types of *memory trace structures* in the episodic memory system. According to the second interpretation, the retrieval process model, only simple copies of the item are encoded in episodic memory, but this model postulates a much more complex set of *retrieval processes*. The experimental data are used to calculate the probabilities of success of the various cue-directed retrieval searches in generating the target item. Both these models provide entirely adequate numerical accounts of the data from experiments which use the reduction method, so it seems impossible to choose between them solely on the basis of experimental data.

Indeed, the difference between the models is not great, but is chiefly one of emphasis. For the ESP-based model, the emphasis is on elaborate *encoding* processes resulting in a fairly complicated memory trace structure, but permitting relatively simple, passive, retrieval operations to match the cues on the trace. For the retrieval process model, the encoding processes are not elaborative and result in a much less complicated memory trace, but the emphasis is on much more elaborate retrieval processes. In other words, the models suggest that the hard work, in terms of information processing, is performed at different *stages* in the encoding–storage–retrieval system (Figure 3.1). The ESP concentrates on encoding processes; the retrieval process model concentrates on retrieval processes. The reason why it is so difficult to decide between these two competing models is that we are only able to observe the inputs and outputs of this information-processing system. The intermediate encoding and retrieval stages are not directly available to us, so we cannot directly attribute results to one stage or another. It is almost always the case, as in the example above, that alternative models give equally adequate accounts of the data: each approach begins with different axioms about how the memory system works; yet both end up with adequate accounts of the data.

Summary of Section 4

- It is implausible that single words are encoded with large and varied amounts of extraneous information in order to support cued recall as the ESP requires.
- Active retrieval processes may take place which could access memory traces without requiring a match between cue information and information already encoded on the memory trace.
- As a result, the memory trace can be a simple non-elaborative copy of the presented item, which has a particular chance of being encoded. A cue sets off a search which generates candidates for recall with a particular probability that one of these candidates will be recognized as being the correct target item.
- The retrieval process model can provide an account of the results of the reduction method which fits the data just as well as the ESP's account.
- The unobservable nature of encoding and retrieval operations makes it difficult to decide between the two approaches on the basis of experimental data.

5   *Empirical tests*

So far we have only considered the rationale of the reduction method and its capability of calculating either the memory trace structure in the memory system (for the ESP model) or the chance of success of certain cue-directed retrieval searches (in the retrieval process model). We haven't really considered how these results might give us further insights into the operation of the episodic memory system. The real benefits of the reduction method analysis come when the experiment, instead of being a simple, two-cue test as you have tried in Activity 1, incorporates further manipulations to see how those manipulations affect encoding, storage or recall.

In just the same way, Newton's laws of motion were useful only when they were applied to the analysis of the motion of heavenly bodies, and were used to create new theoretical explanations for previously documented phenomena like the elliptical orbits of the planets around the sun.

SAQ 17
What manipulations can you think of which might be useful in studying the memory system? HINT: Think of manipulations used in Part II, Section 3.

We will look at three examples of the way the reduction method has been used.

5.1   *Effects of context*

The first is an experiment performed by Tulving and Watkins (1975) as an illustration of the reduction method which they set forth in that article.

TECHNIQUES BOX O

Tulving and Watkins (1975)

Rationale
Tulving and Watkins' experiment was designed to find out how much context affected the structure of the memory trace, as deduced by the reduction method and in line with the Encoding Specificity Principle. Their idea was that context would influence encoding in much the same way as the orienting tasks described in Part II. Tulving and Watkins' prediction was that different contexts would produce different quantities of the various types of memory trace structure, so that a rhyme context would favour the creation of memory traces with rhyme cues encoded

---

on them, and an associate context would favour the creation of memory traces with associate cues encoded on them. (They did not consider a retrieval process model because of their firm allegiance to the ESP.)

Method
The experiment used two conditions of context. Each word which was to be remembered had a context word printed alongside, which was either a word which rhymed with the target, or a word which was associated with the target. The cues given at recall were also rhymes and associates of the targets, but were *different* rhymes and associates to those presented along with the target word. The words which were presented with the targets therefore only provided a *context*. They were not used as cues in the recall tests.

In the experiment, 6 lists of 16 words were presented, each accompanied by a *context* word. Each pair was presented individually to form a separate event or episode. As an example, take the stimulus item CHAIR. The subjects knew that this was a word to be recalled (a target) because it was printed in capital letters (see Table 3.13). The context word was printed alongside the target, and it was either a word which rhymed with the target, e.g. *pear*, or a word that was associated with the target, e.g. *desk*. Each word appeared once for each subject with one type of context, but of course, the counterbalancing meant that each word was presented with both contexts, but to different subjects. The cued recall consisted of using other rhyme and associate words which were *not* the same as the context words themselves, so the rhyme cue for CHAIR would be *hare*, and the associate cue would be *table*. Each cue was identified by words such as 'rhymes with' or 'associated with', e.g. 'hare (rhymes with) . . . ' Half the subjects saw one order of these cues for a given item, and the other half the other order.

Table 3.13

Presentation		Recall	
Context	Target	Cue 1	Cue 2
pear	CHAIR	desk (associated with)	hare (rhymes with)
calf	LAMB	jam (rhymes with)	sheep (associated with)

In these examples, the target CHAIR has been presented with a rhyming context and the word LAMB has been presented with an associate context. The cues for each list of 16 words in any list would be mixed up so that the subject was cued once for each target before the second cues were used.

Another group of subjects would have had the same cues but the target words would have had different contexts (Table 3.14).

125

Table 3.14

Presentation		Recall	
Context	Target	Cue 1	Cue 2
table	CHAIR	desk (associated with)	hare (rhymes with)
tram	LAMB	jam (rhymes with)	sheep (associated with)

A total of 64 subjects learnt the lists and the design was fully counterbalanced. The data was scored in the usual way for the reduction method, and the occurrence of trace types calculated, except that the scoring was performed separately for the different contexts, so that one set of scores represented results obtained when targets had a rhyme word context, and the other set was the result from items which had an associate context.

Results
Table 3.15

		Associate context at presentation		Rhyme context at presentation	
		Rhyme cue		Rhyme cue	
		Success	Failure	Success	Failure
Associate cue	Success	31%	20%	27%	16%
Associate cue	Failure	14%	35%	17%	40%

Using the ESP approach to the reduction method, Tulving and Watkins interpreted these results as occurrences of trace types:

Table 3.16

Associate context at presentation		Rhyme context at presentation	
Type of trace structure	Occurrence	Type of trace structure	Occurrence
AR	31%	AR	27%
A	20%	A	16%
R	14%	R	17%
null	35%	null	40%

Tulving and Watkins considered that these results supported their prediction that different contexts, either Associate or Rhyme, altered the probabilities of occurrence of the various trace types. In particular, it is clear that the memory trace structure with associate information but no rhyme information (structure A), accounted for 20% of recall when an associate context was presented along with the target but accounted for only 16% of recall when a rhyme context was presented along with the target. The memory trace structure with rhyme information but no associate information (structure R), accounted for 14% of recall when an associate word was the context and increased to 17% of recall when a rhyme word was the context.

This is exactly what would be predicted from the ESP, since you would expect that a rhyme context, in contrast to an associate context, would favour the encoding of a memory trace with rhyme information and inhibit the encoding of associate information. This means that the existence of a rhyme cue, for example, biases people towards encoding memory traces with rhymes of the target encoded on them. Since recall depends on the encoding of this specific cue information, this predicts the results we see, and Tulving and Watkins took this positive result to be a corroboration of the ESP, particularly because they allowed no other interpretation. But it is possible, though perhaps less plausible, to interpret these results from a retrieval process point of view.

From the tables of results, it is possible to calculate values for the retrieval process model, namely the probability that the target item itself was encoded (T_r) and the probabilities that the attempt to generate the target from the cues would be successful (A_s and R_s).

Table 3.17

Associate context at presentation		Rhyme context at presentation	
T_r	74%	T_r	70%
R_s	60%	R_s	63%
A_s	69%	A_s	61%

These figures show that, with different contexts, the chance of success in the retrieval search alters. The success rate with the rhyme directed retrieval search (R_s) is 63% when the context word presented with the target is also a rhyme, but drops to 60% when the context is an associate word. The success rate for the associate directed retrieval search (A_s) is 69% when the context is an associate word, but drops to 61% when the context is a rhyme.

It may not be immediately obvious why the performance of retrieval searches should alter because of encoding conditions, but it is important to remember that the encoding context conditions consist of context words which themselves reflect the relationship of the cue to the target. For example, when the context word for CHAIR is *desk* then it is quite possible that CHAIR may have been encoded with *desk* on the memory trace as well. So when the retrieval cue *table* is given, its chance of success is enhanced because it effectively has *two* chances at generating a match to the memory trace, since the cue word *table* is associated with both the words which have been encoded. The search can access the trace either by generating CHAIR directly or by generating the word *desk*, which can then retrieve the trace. The same argument applies to the rhyme context.

Now you might say that the retrieval process model has been forced to concede that it is the difference in the *encodings* of the trace which produces the differences in retrieval. So what is the difference in the models and why not simply accept the ESP model lock, stock and barrel? In fact, the retrieval process model has stuck to its principle that the connexion between the cue *table* and the target CHAIR is only made at retrieval by the generation process. The encoded memory trace is *not* an *elaboration* of the presented stimulus which would include other associated words like *table* which were not presented. The ESP model does require that the encoding resulted in *table* being encoded on the memory trace in order that *table* should be able to work as a cue.

The main difference is the stage at which these elaborations are carried out. The ESP claims that all the elaborations are done at encoding; the retrieval process model claims that it is all done at retrieval. While experiments like Tulving and Watkins' minimize the differences between the two models, we shall see in further experiments that the differences between the two models can be more glaring. Incidentally, you may have noticed that the probability of a memory trace of the item itself being encoded in the retrieval process model falls from 74% for words presented with associate contexts to 70% for words presented with rhyme contexts. This change reflects a difference in successful recall to both cues with different contexts which is explained by neither model.

5.2   Effects of delay

The next experiment we look at was reported by Ogilvie, Tulving, Paskowitz and Jones (1980). Here the factor that was manipulated was the length of delay before recall was tested.

TECHNIQUES BOX P

Ogilvie, Tulving, Paskowitz and Jones (1980)

Rationale
Ogilvie *et al.* expected that memory traces (as identified by the ESP) may disintegrate over time. So, at longer delays between presentation and recall, what was once a large, composite elaborate trace would fragment into simpler traces which would not support recall to so many cues. For example, a trace which starts life with both associate and rhyme cue information on it (an AR trace) may break up, leaving behind a trace with only rhyme cue information on it (an R trace) or may disintegrate still further to a null trace, capable of supporting no recall.

Method
A list of 48 single words were presented one at a time. Three types of cues were used: an associate of the word, a rhyme, and a third cue described by the authors as a *copy cue* (to which we will return below). Recall of half the list was tested after a short delay and recall of the other half after a longer delay.

Results
Although Ogilvie *et al.* used three cues in their experiment, we will first look at the results for just rhyme and associate cues.

Table 3.18

| | | Short delay | | | | Long delay | |
| | | Rhyme cue | | | | Rhyme cue | |
		Success	Failure			Success	Failure
Associate cue	Success	15%	31%	Associate cue	Success	21%	18%
	Failure	8%	46%		Failure	9%	52%

As in the previous experiments, these results can be interpreted directly as demonstrating the proportions of different trace structures. This is shown in Table 3.19 overleaf.

Surprisingly, rather than the number of complete traces declining over time, there are actually *more* complete traces (more words recalled to both cues) after a long delay than after a short delay (15% complete traces rose to 21%). These results are entirely at odds with what was expected. The fact that memory traces were apparently being *created*

Table 3.19

Short delay		Long delay	
Type of trace structure	Probability of occurrence	Type of trace structure	Probability of occurrence
AR	15%	AR	21%
A	31%	A	18%
R	8%	R	9%
null	46%	null	52%

when they should have been lost, while perhaps not impossible, doesn't fit in with any theory of memory so far advanced, and doesn't seem to make a lot of sense. How has this strange state of affairs come about? In this case, a glance at the results of the retrieval process analysis may shed some light:

Table 3.20

Short delay		Long delay	
T_r	72%	T_r	55%
R_s	32%	R_s	55%
A_s	64%	A_s	71%

We see that, according to this analysis, the number of memory traces for the items themselves has actually gone down over the delay, from 72% to 55%, as most theories of memory would predict. What has gone up, however, are the probabilities of success in the retrieval searches. In the case of the search directed by the rhyme cue, this improved from a 32% chance of success to a 55% chance of success, while the search directed by the associate cue improved from 64% to 71%. What has produced these improvements? Shouldn't a retrieval search generating candidates for recall have a fixed or constant chance of success? Why should the ability of the subject to generate appropriate candidates from the cues improve over time?

5.3   Retrieval as a skill

It turns out that this experiment differed in an important respect from that of Tulving and Watkins (1975) discussed in Techniques Box N. Tulving and Watkins identified each cue as it was presented, by a phrase like 'rhymes with' or 'associated with', whereas Ogilvie *et al.* did not tell the subjects which cue was which. And remember there were three cues used in this experiment (we shall look at the third cue shortly). Also, the subjects had done no similar experiments before, and were given no practice. This being so, it seems quite likely that what happened in this experiment was that subjects improved because they gradually learnt the best ways to handle the recall cues as they worked through successive trials.

In Ogilvie *et al.*'s experiment, memory traces of items were being lost from storage during the long delay (T_r decreases over time) as would be expected. However, the increase in efficiency of the retrieval searches more than makes up for this decline so that the subjects are able to remember more items after a delay than they could before (R_s and A_s increased over the delay). This is a case where the ESP analysis makes little sense of the results, since it does not seem acceptable to consider that memory traces are being created long after presentation has stopped. But the retrieval process analysis reveals that the increasing levels of recall come about despite the loss of memory traces because the active retrieval operations improved so much.

So the differences between the ESP-based trace structure model and the retrieval process model make a considerable difference to how the two models *make sense* of a set of results. This is an important lesson about how models of memory are evaluated. Both these models are capable of producing entirely adequate *numerical* accounts of the data. Neither fits the data better than the other, and you can't do a statistical test to tell which is a better model. But when you look at the way they explain and give meaning to the results, and how those explanations fit into what we already know or think about the psychology of the human information processing system, then it is possible to evaluate the advantages and disadvantages that one model may have over the other.

Summary of Section 5

- Changing the context of stimulus items affects the way they are recalled. The ESP interprets this as a change in the encoding of the memory trace to favour certain types of information. The retrieval process interpretation is that the efficiency of retrieval searches has changed, but concedes that this is due to the different encodings of the two contexts.
- Under some circumstances, *total* recall appears to improve over a time delay. The ESP has to accommodate this result by postulating that memory traces are being created long after the items have been presented. The retrieval process interpretation is

that subjects recall more despite the normal loss of items from memory, because this is offset as they learn to use better retrieval strategies during recall.

● Since both models account for the data equally well numerically, deciding which model is the most appropriate depends on which interpretation makes the most psychological sense.

6 *Recognition*

Have you ever had the embarrassing experience of meeting someone who obviously recognizes you, sometimes in an overtly friendly way, yet you do not recognize them at all and they may not even look in the slightest bit familiar? And have these hopefully rare encounters sometimes been resolved when the person in question mentions some key words, perhaps a common experience like a holiday or name, which immediately gives you total recall of who he or she is and when you met each other? This failure of recognition is by no means rare and is easily simulated in the laboratory by a simple experiment, as demonstrated by Activity 2.

Activity 2
Read through the following list of word pairs taking about half a minute overall for the whole list. Don't waste your time trying to remember the list perfectly: perfect recall always spoils memory experiments! You should then continue reading the text, as the activity relies on a delay between presentation and test in order to work.

hope	– HIGH
stem	– SHORT
whisky	– WATER
moth	– FOOD
cabbage	– ROUND
glass	– HARD
country	– OPEN
tool	– HAND
memory	– SLOW
covering	– COAT
barn	– DIRTY
spider	– BIRD
crust	– CAKE
deep	– SLEEP

train	– BLACK
mountain	– TREE
cottage	– LOVE
art	– GIRL
adult	– WORK
brave	– WEAK
door	– RED
roll	– RUG
think	– STUPID
exist	– BEING

6.1   Copy cues

Now let's look at the third cue used by Ogilvie *et al.* (1980). The cue they used was really quite intriguing, because it was quite unlike the other two cues. It was a direct *copy* of the original stimulus. So the cue for the word CHAIR was, simply, 'CHAIR'. Ogilvie *et al.* refer to it as the *copy cue*. The subject was supposed to respond to this cue by writing down the word CHAIR next to its copy. Why did Ogilvie *et al.* use such a cue?

The answer stems largely from their adherence to the Encoding Specificity Principle. In the ESP approach, the copy cue is simply another source of information which may support retrieval if it is specifically encoded on the episodic memory trace. There is no *a priori* reason in this approach to treat it any differently from other cues. Remember, subjects were not told which cue was which during the tests.

By using the reduction method (suitably adapted for handling three recall cues) to measure the trace structure, the ESP-based model comes up with results like those in Table 3.21 overleaf (C represents the existence of Copy cue information on the memory trace).

Now we see that there are eight different possible types of memory trace. A complete trace (structure ARC) can support recall to any of the three cues. Next there are three trace structures with different combinations of information which will support recall to two of the cues, three trace structures which support recall to only one cue, and of course a trace type which supports no recall at all (null).

In theory, the reduction method can be extended to analyse any number of cues, producing trace structures of increasing complexity, but in practice there is a limit to the number of cues that people can handle in experiments like this. Perhaps you can appreciate how difficult it must have been for subjects faced with long lists of recall cues, and not knowing to which class each cue belongs.

Table 3.21

Short delay		Long delay	
Type of trace structure	Occurrence	Type of trace structure	Occurrence
ARC	16%	ARC	20%
AC	31%	AC	13%
AR	−1%	AR	0%
CR	4%	CR	7%
A	7%	A	4%
C	14%	C	18%
R	3%	R	3%
null	26%	null	34%

The change in performance by subjects as they go through Ogilvie *et al*'s pretty gruelling test procedures again shows up as anomalies for the ESP model. As Table 3.21 shows, the number of complete memory traces (structure ARC) appears to *rise* over the delay interval (from 16% to 20%) in opposition to the expected decline. The retrieval process analysis of these data estimates that the proportion of memory traces actually declines from 77% to 70%, although the overall level of retrieval does rise. The test sequence for the three cues is so long (10 minutes) that it seems quite plausible that subjects are learning how to use the cues as they progress through the tests.

Now turn to the testing part of Activity 2 on p. 151.

You should find that there are some items in the recognition test which you did not recognize as 'old' items you had seen before, while in the later recall test you were able to remember them.

The name for this inability to identify items in a recognition test which may be later recalled is known as the *recognition failure of recallable words;* but the name is normally abbreviated to *recognition failure*. This phenomenon is of great importance to our understanding of memory, as it has a quite different impact on different theories.

This recognition failure is an experimental analogue of the everyday situation described at the start of this section. In both situations, you are confronted with an input cue (e.g. a person's face) which you have seen in the past, yet are unable to recognize it. But later, when more of the original context is provided, you are able to recall the stimuli.

In the case of the unrecognized face, your memory may be jolted (cued) by a key fact. In Activity 2 you could recall unrecognized words when given cues. So the original failure to recognize cannot have been due to simple loss of the memory trace since the episodic memory was available to be recalled by other cues.

SAQ 18
Think about Activity 2.
(a) What two tests were used in this experiment?
(b) What cues were used in each of those tests?
(c) What is the main point of experiments like Activity 2?
(d) What is the phenomenon demonstrated called?
(e) How is that experiment related to the reduction method described above?

6.2   *Recognition as a copy cue*

If we look back at Ogilvie *et al*'s experiment, we can observe the existence of two memory trace structures: A and R. These traces support recall of the target word to either the associate cue or the rhyme cue but *not* to the copy cue. In that experiment, when the data is examined carefully, there are in fact several instances where the copy cue fails to retrieve the item but the associate or rhyme cue succeeds. What does this mean in practice?

It means that, while the subject is able to recall and even write down the word CHAIR to a cue like *table*, and therefore must have some knowledge about the word, yet when faced with the cue word CHAIR as a 'copy' of the original target she is *unable* to identify it as a word originally presented to her! The subject has failed to recognize the cue word CHAIR as a copy of the original target item although she can recall the word to a different cue. We can see that what the subject is asked to do with a copy cue is to *recognize* the word as one that was presented in the original list.

Activity 2 is in fact a special case of the reduction method. In the recognition test copy cues are supplied and you are asked to *recognize* those copies as such. In the recall test, associate cues are supplied and you are asked to *recall* the original target items. The focal point of the procedure is the discovery of items, usually several if the conditions are right, which you were *unable* to recognize in the first test, but yet were able to remember in a recall test. Most of you should have found that there was at least one item that you did not identify in the recognition test yet could recall later, although to be absolutely certain that this will happen, the delay from reading the stimulus items to starting the recognition test needs to be about three minutes, and is usually at least five minutes. Techniques Box Q shows how the reduction method can be applied to recognition failure experiments.

TECHNIQUES BOX Q

Recognition Failure Experiments

Rationale
The aim is to measure the level of recognition failure of recallable words under varying conditions.

Method
Subjects are presented with a list of paired items. The items can be of any form but are usually words or sentences. One member of the pair is designated the *target* and the other the *context*. Each pair is presented individually to constitute an individual event or episode. After presentation, there may be an intervening interfering task of any length (delays up to several days have been used). The testing sequence consists of a recognition test presented first, in which the targets ('old' items) are presented mixed up with a set of distractors ('new' items). Subjects have to attempt to identify as many targets as they can without, obviously, incorrectly identifying distractors as targets. Sometimes the test may be a forced-choice test, in which each target is presented with three or four distractors, and subjects have to pick out which one was the target. After this test a cued recall test is given in which the *context* item is presented as a cue for recall of the *target*.

Presentation		Recognition test		Cued recall	
Context	Target	Target	Distractors	Context cue	Target
train	BLACK	BLACK	GREEN CHALK	train	....

Results
The numbers of items recalled in both tests, one test but not the other, and not recalled at all are entered in a 2 × 2 table, just as in the reduction method. The critical data are the number of items recalled but not recognized (which demonstrate *recognition failure*). Because this is the major focus of interest, only one order of tests is used (we are not interested in the level of recognition once recall has failed).

Table 3.22

		Cued recall test	
		Success	Failure
Recognition test	Success	14%	20%
	Failure	7%	59%

In this example table of results, the critical data is the proportion of items which were recalled but not recognized (in this case 7%).

6.3   Impact of recognition failure on the generate–recognize theory of recall

The discussion of the retrieval process model of recall has introduced the idea of a generate–recognize theory of recall. In this model, recall always involves two stages. These are:

1 The *generation* of candidates for recall via a set of complex retrieval processes; and
2 The *recognition* of one of these candidates as a target item.

The crucial aspect of this model is that *both* of these operations must succeed if recall is to succeed. Now the second stage of the recall process is a recognition judgment, just like that in the recognition test itself. So if the recognition judgment fails in a recognition test, how is it able to succeed later when it forms part of the recall process? In other words, if the recognition judgment is going to fail, recall ought to fail also. Therefore, the generate–recognize theory of recall predicts that recognition failure of recallable words should never occur, or at least it should be very rare. But not only is recognition failure widespread and very reliable, it is also possible under some conditions to have levels of recall *greater* than the level of recognition. It seems therefore that these results are very damaging to generate–recognize theories of recall.

6.4   The ESP explanation of recognition failure

ESP-based models have no difficulty coping with this phenomenon. Indeed, it was largely this phenomenon that shaped the birth and development of the ESP itself. This approach makes no distinction between recognition and cued recall; they are both simply cases of cued recall of a memory trace. The main difference is essentially the particular type of cue used. The recognition test uses 'copy cues', while the recall test uses 'associate' or 'rhyme' cues. So the ESP places no limit on the amount of recognition failure which may occur, since the various types of memory trace structure can easily include cases where associate or rhyme cues are effective but the copy cue is not.

This produces the rather curious possibility of a memory trace being encoded which appears to lack information corresponding to the copy cue yet has information capable of supporting recall to other cues! Perhaps the best way to think about this strange state of affairs is that the original encoding, which according to the ESP model produces a great deal of elaboration and alteration, may have so distorted the representation of the target that it is no longer matched by a copy cue. Other cues, however, may be much more closely related to the information encoded on the trace.

In other words, the retrieval cues, whether associate, rhyme or copy, act completely independently when retrieving the trace, and no restrictions are placed on either cue's chance of success according to the success or failure of the other cue. If no trace exists at all, all types of cues will have to fail, which introduces a small correlation between recognition and recall.

6.5   Mandler's dual process model of recognition

Another theory which attempts to explain recognition failure was proposed by Rabinowitz, Mandler and Barsalou (1977), based on a theory of memory developed by Mandler. In his theory there is more than one encoding of the stimulus. At encoding, two traces or *codes* are laid down.

1 The *presentation code*. The presentation code of an item is the encoding of the *general* context of the item. This includes various physical properties or perceptual features of the stimulus such as its brightness, clarity, colour etc.

2 The *conceptual code*. The conceptual code of an item is a representation of the *association* between items which results from their being presented together. In the case of the context and target pairs of words which are presented in recognition failure experiments, it is the conceptual code which represents the *relational information* which links the two words in memory. In other words, in this model the words are linked together by associations which are encoded on the conceptual code.

Cued recall operates by retrieving the conceptual code, because only this code has the relational information which allows the cue to access and identify the target.

Recognition can occur in either of two ways:

1 Immediate and automatic access to the presentation code. The presentation code for the item (e.g. TRAIN) is subjected to a kind of *familiarity judgment*, in which the perceptual properties of the stimulus which have been encoded are evaluated and a judgement is made as to whether that word seems familiar enough to have been presented to the subject in the list under test. If this evaluation exceeds a chosen criterion, the item is recognized and no further processing is required. If the evaluation of familiarity is very low so that it falls *below* another chosen criterion, the subject may consider that the item is so unfamiliar that he may immediately classify the target as 'new'. But, if the familiarity is judged to be between these two criteria the recognition process proceeds to a second evaluation.

2 This second evaluation abandons the presentation code and the target (TRAIN) is used as a retrieval cue in an attempt to access the conceptual code. If this retrieval attempt succeeds, the item is then recognized as old.

Recognition failure can occur in the first evaluation because items have a very low familiarity value. But according to Rabinowitz *et al.*, when recognition failure is frequent it stems from the second evaluation and is due to *asymmetries* in the conceptual code. If we look at a presented pair like '*black* TRAIN', there is not just one *relational link* between the words according to this theory, but two, one from *black* to TRAIN and the other from TRAIN to *black*. Suppose the target item TRAIN is being recognized. In the recognition process, if the processing of the presentation code fails to come up with a definitive answer, the second stage attempts to access the conceptual code using the word TRAIN as a cue. In other words, the process investigates the existence of a link *from* TRAIN *to black* in the conceptual code. If this access attempt succeeds at retrieving a conceptual code, then the item is successfully recognized, and that resolves the problem of the presentation code not being sufficiently strong to give an immediate result to the recognition judgment.

For the cued recall test, however, it is the word *black* which is given as a cue for retrieval of the conceptual code, which explores the existence of a link from *black* to TRAIN. Rabinowitz *et al.* claim that this access can succeed while the other fails, and that most recognition failure is due to this asymmetry. Thus, recognition fails because:

1 The familiarity value of the presentation code for TRAIN is not high enough to permit identification; and
2 There is no link in the conceptual code which goes *from* TRAIN *to black*.

But recall succeeds because there is a link from *black* to TRAIN. Thus we can explain the recognition failure of recallable words.

As evidence in support of this, they ran experiments which modified the normal recognition failure procedure by changing the cued recall test to use TRAIN as the cue for recall of *black*, rather than the other way round. In these circumstances, the recall attempt made in the recognition process uses the same cue (e.g. TRAIN) for retrieval of the conceptual code as the cued recall test, so recognition failure, where it is due to asymmetries in the conceptual code, should largely disappear. In their experiment, Rabinowitz *et al.* did find very little recognition failure. However, the power of their conclusions was undermined by an experiment by Le Voi and Rawles (1979) which showed that, at longer delays (about 20 minutes) between presentation of the list and the recognition test, there were large amounts of recognition failure which could not be accounted for by their model.

6.6 Kintsch's theory: 'generate–recognize' reborn

An analysis by Kintsch (1978) showed that recognition failure could be explained by a modified form of the generate–recognize model, the very theoretical approach thought to be falsified by the recognition failure phenomenon! In the generate–recognize model, unlike the two-stage recognition process which we saw in Mandler's model, it is recall which is a two-stage process, since it requires first the *generation* of candidates for recall followed by *recognition* of the candidates as the target. Kintsch's modification was to reject the assumption that the recognition judgment performed in the *recall* test operates to the same *criterion* as that in the recognition test. In other words, subjects are happy to accept items as 'old' in the recall test which they would normally reject in the recognition test. That is, in the recall test, subjects may be happy to remember anything at all and apply a weak criterion, but in the true recognition test they may be much more cautious.

Suppose we look at the presented pair *black* TRAIN. The word TRAIN may produce a familiarity value of 2. What Kintsch is saying, is that in a recognition test, the subject sets a high criterion for the recognition judgment, such as 3, in order to be confident that he really has seen the item under test in the list. Because TRAIN has a familiarity value of only 2, it will not be recognized. But in the recall test, the subject changes this criterion for a lower, weaker one, such as 1, perhaps because he is not so concerned about the prospect of making an error. If TRAIN is successfully generated, as a candidate response to the cue *black*, then its familiarity value (2) exceeds the new criterion in the recognition judgment and the subject accepts it and produces it in recall. So the subject fails to *recognize* items because the familiarity value is below the higher criterion, but may still *recall* them to cues because the familiarity value is above the lower criterion.

Thus in Kintsch's model, the process of recognition has different criteria depending on whether the task is a recognition or cued recall test. The model is especially useful, since it is possible to calculate for each experiment the exact amount by which the two criteria differ, which means it is then possible to investigate whether changes in these criteria can be manipulated experimentally.

6.7 Jones' theory: dual routes to recall

Another explanation of the phenomenon is that advanced by G. Jones (1978). In this model, recognition is a single process, just as in Kintsch's model. Jones' model differs in that it specifies that there are not one but *two* quite separate and independent ways to remember information in the cued recall test.

1 The first is another resurrection of the generate–recognize model, in which the attempt to recall an item is by means of a search process, which is followed by a recognition judgment to check its validity. Unlike Kintsch's adaptation, however, this recognition judgment is *exactly* the same as that in the recognition test proper, such that if an item is recognized in one test it *must* be recognized in the other.

2 The second recall process is more like that in the ESP approach, in that the process works by making a direct match between the cue and memory traces. If the cue correctly matches information in the trace, that trace is immediately retrieved without recourse to a further recognition test. This is in fact direct access retrieval just like that used in the ESP model.

Although these two recall routes are quite independent and can occur in any order, it is probably easier to consider the second, direct access route being used first and the generate–recognize route only being attempted when direct access retrieval fails. The novel aspect of Jones' model is that it allows more than one way of recalling things.

Although Mandler's theory had two forms of encoding (presentation code and conceptual code), the presentation code was only useful for recognition and played no part in cued recall. In cued recall, only the conceptual code was any use and the retrieval attempt was a single attempt at retrieving the relational information from the cue to the target. In fact, most older theories of recall consider only one retrieval process, usually on the grounds of simplicity. However, Jones' model, despite two retrieval mechanisms, is not more complicated than Kintsch's model. Kintsch's model is complicated by the way the criterion in the recognition judgement varies between the memory tests (dual criterion), whereas Jones' model specifies that the recognition test always has the same criterion, but has *dual recall routes*. It combines the idea of direct access recall as used in the ESP model with the idea that when that fails, subjects can carry on generating new possibilities for a response which, if those new candidates are recognized as targets, can then be successfully recalled.

Jones' model explains recognition failure, because the direct-access retrieval route (in which the cue is compared directly with the memory trace) does not require recognition. Thus items can be recalled for which the recognition test may fail.

6.8 Intrinsic and extrinsic recall

We are now seeing more clearly the way that cues may operate to achieve recall. One further distinction needs to be drawn. Jones' two routes to recall are really like two separate models of recall. His generate–recognize route is very like the original form of generate–recognize theories, and his direct-access route looks very like the model of recall based on the Encoding Specificity Principle set out above. Does this mean we *have* to accept the ESP, and that two recall routes are *always* potentially available to us?

No, we do not. The dual route model was particularly useful in explaining the recognition failure phenomenon. But let's take another look at the experimental set-up (Techniques Box Q). The stimuli in this experiment (as used in Activity 2) consists of pairs of words, e.g. *black* TRAIN. The recognition test in this case is a test for recognition of TRAIN on its own, but more importantly the *recall* test uses the *same* word (*black*) that was originally presented along with the target TRAIN. So the cue used in the recall test *was identical to a word presented with the target item itself*. In this case, the cue information is said to be *intrinsic* to (contained within) the original stimulus. It is possible, therefore, that recall works by direct access in which intrinsic cues are directly matched with traces, and this *intrinsic recall route* can only work when the original stimuli included information which *directly* corresponded with that of the cue.

If we now return to the kind of experiment you did in Activity 1, in those experiments, the cues were *not* presented with the stimulus words. In the original list BALL was presented alone, so the cue *tennis* never appeared with it in the presentation list. In this case the cue information is said to be *extrinsic* to the stimulus (target) item.

It is possible, therefore, that the direct access intrinsic recall route was not available in this experiment. If that is so, the only remaining route would be the generate–recognize *extrinsic recall route*, which as we saw formed the basis for the retrieval process model discussed in Section 4 as an explanation of results obtained using the reduction method.

This underlines the crucial difference between Jones and the ESP approach. The direct access recall route proposed by Jones is very similar to the ESP, in that recall can *only* succeed by that route if, and only if, information about the cue was encoded on the memory trace. But the model does *not* specify that *all* recall *must* use that route. The ESP approach, however, insists that this is the *only* route to recall and that this applies even when the cues to be used were *not* physically presented with the original stimuli, i.e. the ESP maintains that cues can only operate in one way (by direct matching to traces), whether or not they are intrinsic or extrinsic to the original stimulus. For the cues to work, the subject must have encoded an *elaboration* of the stimulus which included all and any cues which could later successfully produce recall. Again, it is very difficult to devise experiments which can allow us to choose one approach rather than the other. Experiments which initially appear to favour one approach, as recognition failure experiments were first thought to support the ESP, can often be explained by other approaches, and in fact can provide quite strong evidence in their favour!

Summary of Section 6

- A *copy cue* is a cue which is a simple copy of the original stimulus. This is just like a recognition test, in which copies of the original stimulus are presented and the subject has to pick them out from a set of distractors.
- It is possible for cued recall to succeed while recognition of the same target items fails, which is the phenomenon of *recognition failure*. This is difficult to explain by a simple generate–recognize model of recall because successful recognition is essential to the recall process, so if recognition cannot succeed neither can recall.
- The ESP explains recognition failure as a natural result of the copy cue simply being another type of cue encoded on the episodic memory trace and capable of failing independently of the success or failure of other cues.
- Mandler's dual process theory considers that recognition failure is a natural result of the failure to recall conceptual codes in the second stage of a two-stage recognition judgment. When this occurs, the conceptual code lacks the relational link from the target to the cue, but can support recall because there is a link from the cue to the target.
- Kintsch's theory considers that recognition failure is a natural result of the recognition judgment using a different, lower criterion in the recognition stage of a two-stage generate–recognize recall process, compared to the higher criterion used in the (single-stage) recognition test.
- Jones' theory considers that recall can occur through two routes, a direct access recall route and a generate–recognize recall route. Recognition failure results when the direct access route to recall (which does not require any recognition) succeeds, but the recognition judgment fails.
- Table 3.23 overleaf summarizes the models discussed in this Part.

Table 3.23 Comparison of models

	ESP	Retrieval process	Kintsch	Mandler	Jones
Encoding	elaborate trace structure	simple copy	simple copy	presentation and conceptual codes	simple copy
Recognition	direct access (using copy cue)	familiarity judgment (fixed criterion)	familiarity judgment (high criterion)	familiarity judgment possibly followed by retrieval access test	familiarity judgment (fixed criterion)
Intrinsic cued recall	direct access retrieval	generation of candidate followed by recognition	generation of candidate followed by recognition (low criterion)	direct access of conceptual code	direct access of memory trace possibly with additional generate-recognize retrieval attempt
Extrinsic cued recall	direct access retrieval	generation of candidate followed by recognition	generation of candidate followed by recognition (low criterion)	possibly generate-recognize?	generate-recognize retrieval route

7   The status of cued recall: a recapitulation

Cued recall, as I pointed out in the introduction, is considered to be a basic process in memory. Yet we can see that providing explicit cues for recall of items does not unambiguously allow us to interpret the results of recall. Tulving's Encoding Specificity Principle would have us believe that, when a retrieval cue operates, it provides a direct match to the episodic memory trace. If recall succeeds, then we conclude that when the memory trace was encoded, it must have incorporated information which matches that provided by our chosen cue. If there is no overlap between the cue and the memory trace, retrieval cannot occur.

But we have seen that there is another way the cue could act. The subject, armed with the knowledge that the cue rhymes with or is associated with a list word, can use it to direct her own interrogation of the memory store, generating a set of candidates which are then matched with information in the store for identification as targets. We have seen that this active creation of candidates, followed by an evaluation of their verity, is the basis of a generate–recognize model of recall, in which the generation of new candidates are compared with stored items in a recognition test.

So there are two ideas about the way cues act, which we can refer to as the intrinsic and extrinsic action of cues. The first assumes that the information represented by successful cues is *intrinsic* (contained *within* the memory trace), allowing the cue's information to match directly with information on the trace to effect retrieval. This is the kind of recall which the Encoding Specificity Principle uses. In the generate–recognize model, the information in the cue is unrelated to the memory trace, and does not overlap with it. This *extrinsic* information may be used to direct a retrieval process which allows access to the trace for comparison and/or recognition.

The intrinsic recall of the ESP generalizes immediately to recognition. The recognition test simply provides another cue which may give access to the memory trace to effect retrieval. The theory is not damaged by the fact that some cues, even copy cues, may fail when others succeed. But recognition failure is disturbing to the generate–recognize theory of recall, because it does not make sense to suppose that a retrieval process which invokes a recognition judgment as part of its action can succeed when that recognition judgment has previously been shown to fail. But Kintsch showed that it is possible to 'patch up' generate–recognize theory by adopting a different, lower criterion for the recognition judgment in the recall test, so that some items can slip through and be recalled despite the previous failure to recognize them.

Given the obvious difficulty in choosing between these models, it is hardly surprising that someone thought up the idea that they are both correct. Jones' idea is that, when presented with a cue, the retrieval system may attempt to make an immediate match to see if the cue is intrinsically related to a memory trace. If that succeeds, then retrieval has occurred and no more retrieval effort is required. In this case, recall may succeed even though recognition fails. But if it fails, all is not lost, and our cognitive system, one of the most adaptive and flexible systems on earth, is capable of treating the presented cue as extrinsic information which can be used to generate more cues for comparison with traces in the memory system. And that comparison may involve a recognition judgment identical to that performed in the recognition test itself.

7.1   Conclusion

As I write, it is 95 years since William James so eloquently pointed out the central importance of cues to the operation of retrieval from memory. In that time, have we got anywhere, since we seem to be left with possibilities between which we cannot decide, and questions we cannot answer? Part II ended with the truism that good research raises more questions than it answers, which is certainly the situation in all areas of memory research. But, although we have no final answers to these problems, we are much better armed to tackle them than we were before.

Part III has examined in great detail a narrow area of research which has attempted to answer one or two detailed questions about the operation of memory. But even from the above examination of the issues, which represents only a tiny fraction of the current research into cued recall and recognition, we have a clear idea of exactly the kind of theory the ESP gives us, the problems it solves, and the questions it leaves. Similarly, we know many of the problems with generate–recognize and retrieval process models of memory. If we wish, we can combine any or all of these ideas with other theoretical models, for instance the levels of processing approach, to see if the *combination* of ideas provides a greater understanding than each part on its own. For example, by using the analysis provided by the reduction method and the ESP to make deductions about the encoding of the memory trace, we can perform experiments, even real-life experiments, which give much greater precision to our understanding of the way depth, or elaboration, or distinctiveness of encoding affect the retentiveness of information as predicted by the levels of processing approach.

The message for the future of memory research is the same as that provided in Part II. Only when all the insights from encoding specificity, generate–recognize and schema models, levels of processing, working memory and studies of everyday memory are combined into a broadly-based theoretical conception which covers all aspects of cognitive activity in memory will we have the beginnings of a comprehensive theory of memory.

Further reading

1 Thomson and Tulving, 1970. A thorough analysis of cued recall.
2 Tulving and Thomson, 1973. One of the original papers from which the ESP grew.
3 Le Voi *et al*, 1983. This paper sets out the rationale of the reduction method for two and three cues, and investigates and contrasts the ESP model and the retrieval process model.
4 Watkins and Gardiner, 1979. Gives a good summary of the generate–recognize theory of recall.

Activity 1

This activity is a memory test for the words you have just read on page 109. The test provides *cues* for recalling the words. There are two types of cue used, associate and rhyme. *Associate cues* are associated with the target word, so that if the word to be remembered is CAR, for example, the cue might be *drive*. A *rhyme cue* for CAR could be *star*. All you need to do is work through the cues listed below, trying to remember a word from the list you have just read and writing it in beside the cue. Each word is cued by an associate cue and a rhyme cue, but you should not try to link cues together. It is important that you should only look at each cue *once*, and *never* go back to a previous cue. If you do, you will spoil the demonstration, so cover the cues you have done with a piece of paper as you work down. If you can't remember a word, go on to the next cue and don't look back.

1	Long	(associated with)	. . . .
2	Pay	(rhymes with)	. . . .
3	Hot	(associated with)	. . . .
4	Glue	(rhymes with)	. . . .
5	Fur	(associated with)	. . . .
6	Tram	(rhymes with)	. . . .
7	Bloom	(associated with)	. . . .
8	Neat	(rhymes with)	. . . .
9	Fruit	(associated with)	. . . .
10	Wall	(rhymes with)	. . . .
11	Bold	(rhymes with)	. . . .
12	Tennis	(associated with)	. . . .
13	Power	(rhymes with)	. . . .
14	Night	(associated with)	. . . .
15	Teach	(rhymes with)	. . . .
16	Sky	(associated with)	. . . .
17	Fort	(rhymes with)	. . . .
18	Bitter	(associated with)	. . . .
19	Moat	(rhymes with)	. . . .
20	Sheep	(associated with)	. . . .

(After you have gone through these cues turn to the next page for scoring.)

Scoring
The correct answers to each cue are given below, with numbers corresponding to the cues in the memory test above. First, work through the answer sheet, circling those which you got right in the text. Remember each word has been cued twice, so you have to check two cues. For example, the word SHORT was the answer for both Cue 1 and Cue 17, so you should check both answers and circle the number if you got it right.

			Condition 1 (Associate cue first)				
						Rhyme cue	
Answer	Associate cue	Rhyme cue				Success	Failure
Short	1	17				A	B
Cold	3	11			Success		
Coat	5	19		Associate cue			
Flower	7	13			Failure	C	D
Peach	9	15					

			Condition 2 (Rhyme cue first)				
						Rhyme cue	
Answer	Rhyme cue	Associate cue				Success	Failure
Day	2	14				V	W
Blue	4	16			Success		
Lamb	6	20		Associate cue			
Sweet	8	18			Failure	X	Y
Ball	10	12					

The next task is to put your scores in the table beside each condition. You have correctly recalled each word either twice, once or never. Looking at each condition separately, fill in the 2 × 2 table on the right. First count up the answers in condition 1 that you remembered to *both* cues. This number goes in Box A. Then count the answers you couldn't remember at all in Condition 1, and put the number in Box D. Then count the times that you remembered the answer to only one of the cues. You should do this twice: once for when you remembered the answer to the rhyme cue but not the associate cue, when the answer goes in C; and again for when you remembered the answer to the associate cue but not the rhyme cue, when the answer goes in B.

149

For example, suppose you remembered COLD to the rhyme cue *bold*, but not to the associate cue *hot*, and you remembered FLOWER to *power* but not to *bloom*, then you will have circled the numbers 11 and 13. If these are the only two words which you could recall to rhyme cues but *not* to associate cues, then you should write 2 in Box C of the table.

Repeat this for Condition 2. The number for both correct goes in V, both wrong in Y, rhyme cue correct but associate cue wrong in X, associate cue correct but rhyme cue wrong in W.

Now convert every figure to a percentage. All you need to do is to multiply every number by 20, and put them into these tables below. As a check, the numbers in each table should add up to 100%.

		Associate cue first Rhyme cue				*Rhyme cue first* Rhyme cue	
		Success	Failure			Success	Failure
	Success	A	B		Success	V	W
Associate cue				Associate cue			
	Failure	C	D		Failure	X	Y

The summary table below is filled in in a special way. Each cell in the summary table is labelled with the corresponding cell which you should use from the two tables above. For example, the bottom left number is entered with the value in the cell labelled C in the table above. The bottom right cell is filled in by taking the average of the two cells D and Y. The cell marked * is calculated by adding up the numbers in the other three cells of the summary table and subtracting from 100%. This way of calculating the cells is a distinctive feature of the reduction method which is explained in the text.

Summary Table

		Rhyme cue	
		Success	Failure
Associate cue	Success	*	W
	Failure	C	$(D+Y) \div 2$

Activity 2

There are two tests in this activity. First go through the list below, circling the items which you *recognize* as having been in the list you read through on pages 132–3.

TREE	WASH	RUG	PAIN	STUPID	HIGH	QUEEN	BLACK
SMOKE	COAT	MAN	CHAIR	BABY	BIRD	GIRL	GO
RED	BUG	WEAK	HARD	NEED	SHORT	BEING	CUT
SHEEP	LOVE	FLOWER	DAY	WORK	WATER	HAND	COLD
CAKE	LIGHT	GREEN	FOOD	LARGE	DIRTY	SWEET	WIND
BALL	OPEN	SLOW	WET	ROUND	SLEEP	BLUE	SMOOTH

Now cover up this list while you do the second test. The second test is *cued recall*. A list of words, in which each word corresponds to one of the words in each pair of the list which you read, is presented. Try to remember *one* word which went with each cue word and write it next to the cue. DO NOT go back to the previous recognition test or you will spoil the demonstration.

hope	. . . .
stem	. . . .
whisky	. . . .
moth	. . . .
cabbage	. . . .
glass	. . . .
country	. . . .
tool	. . . .
memory	. . . .
covering	. . . .
barn	. . . .
spider	. . . .
crust	. . . .
deep	. . . .
train	. . . .
mountain	. . . .
cottage	. . . .
art	. . . .
adult	. . . .
brave	. . . .
door	. . . .
roll	. . . .
think	. . . .
exist	. . . .

Part III   Encoding and Retrieval

Scoring
Use the list on pages 132–3 to check your answers on the RECALL
test. Now simply see if there are items you recalled which you did NOT
recognize in the first test. This phenomenon is explored in Section 6.1.

Appendix to Part III

To calculate the values for the retrieval-process analysis we use the
table of results of the reduction method:

| | | Rhyme cue | |
		Success	Failure
Associate cue	Success	v	w
	Failure	y	z

The values are calculated as follows:

$$A_s = 1 - \frac{y}{1 - (w + z)}$$

$$R_s = 1 - \frac{w}{1 - (y + z)}$$

$$T_r = \frac{y}{(1 - A_s) \times R_s}$$

Overview

Martin Le Voi

The three parts of this book have taken quite different views of the problem of memory. However, each one has had to tackle the problems of encoding of the memory trace, retrieval and executive control in its own way.

1 Encoding

Starting with encoding operations, we can see that several models of memory have laid a great emphasis on these. The schema models discussed in Part I hold that new experiences are not just passively copied, or recorded into memory. A memory representation is actively constructed by processes that are strongly influenced by pre-existing schemas representing previously acquired knowledge. In this model, the encoding process is a sophisticated system of storing *well-organized* information. The levels-of-processing model introduced in Part II also makes heavy demands on encoding processes. In this approach, the durability and form of memory traces is determined by the depth of processing performed on stimuli and events. If extensive deep processing is carried out, a durable, accessible trace is encoded.

One phenomenon discussed in Part I illustrates this nicely. 'Flashbulb memories' occur in everyday memory when some event triggers an encoding which preserves minute details of the event. The classic example is peoples' memories of events surrounding the assassination of President Kennedy. Many people appear to have highly accurate and persistent memories of this event and the circumstances in which they heard about it; this can be considered to be an encoding phenomenon, in which the highly charged emotional content of the occasion prompted very deep or elaborative processing. The levels of processing approach would predict that this deep or elaborative encoding would produce very durable traces.

The Encoding Specificity Principle (ESP) also emphasizes the importance of encoding, but in a rather different way. Encoding is vital, but the type of encoding (deep or shallow, elaborative or elementary) is not sufficient to determine recall. For retrieval of the memory trace, the cue must reinstate the information present on that trace. In this model, it is the correspondence between the encoding of the stimulus and the retrieval cue which determines recall.

In Part III, an experiment by Tulving and Watkins (1975) is described, which investigated whether rhyme or associate contexts aided recall. According to the levels-of-processing approach, rhyme processing is affected by the physical 'sound' of the word, whereas associate processing is performed at a relatively deeper level which involves word meanings and connections. So the levels-of-processing approach would predict that the associate context should have produced the more durable, better accessed trace. But Tulving and Watkins' results showed that performance depends on whether recall is prompted (cued) by rhyme or associate information, so that best recall occurred when the cue *matched* the encoded information. The requirement that the retrieval cue should be *specifically encoded* on the trace gave the ESP (Encoding Specificity Principle) its name. Finally, in the area of encoding, the experiments by Loftus on eye-witness testimony described in Part I reveal that memory traces can be *recoded* anew to incorporate more, or different, information.

2 Retrieval

Many theories have completely ignored the issue of retrieval operations. Levels-of-processing theory dismisses them with a wave of the hand as being 'probably automatic' (Craik and Lockhart, 1972). ESP plays them down because of its great emphasis on appropriate encoding strategies, but it is at least very explicit about the retrieval operation required, in which the retrieval cue must match with information encoded on the memory trace.

The notion of direct access retrieval is common to many theories. Endemic to ESP, we must also assume that it is the retrieval route required by levels-of-processing theory, in the absence of any firm statement to the contrary. Direct access is used by Mandler's model of episodic memory. The first stage of the recognition judgment is automatic (i.e. direct) access of the presentation code, which is evaluated for familiarity. Recall is also an attempt to access directly the conceptual code in order to examine the associative links contained therein.

Jones' dual recall route model also used direct-access retrieval as a possible route to recall. The other route in Jones' model is the generate–recognize model of retrieval. Recall is produced by generating candidates from the retrieval cue, and these candidates are compared with memory in a recognition test in order to pick out the target. A good example is the experiment by Williams and Hollan (1981) (Part I, p. 52) in which subjects appeared to generate contexts to search for names of their old classmates. Norman and Bobrow's (1979) theory formalized a model of retrieval processes in which a search consisted of going through a cycle of creating cues, generating potential items and evaluating these candidates as genuine targets. This model of retrieval processes is clearly very closely related to the generate–recognize theory discussed in Part III.

This emphasis on active and elaborate retrieval processes may lead us to question the need for *encoding* operations. Much of the organization and active elaboration imposed on memory may not be occurring at encoding at all, but may be produced by reconstructive processes acting at recall (e.g. Part I, Section 4). The difficulty of assigning complex processing to a given stage of memory continues to this day.

Amongst all these models of recall we can see an overall trend emerging. Jones' model of recall is explicitly dual-route, implying that people may choose to use direct access or generate–recognize recall as they see fit. Schema models are unclear as to whether elaborate processing has occurred at encoding (implying simple direct-access retrieval) or at retrieval (implying more complicated retrieval processes). Even Kintsch, after producing a full-blooded defence of generate–recognize models, does not consider it to be the only or even the best model of recall. In the same way, Mandler also acknowledges that direct access recall may be supplemented by generate–recognize models of recall: 'Sometimes we need to generate and subsequently recognize items to complete a memorial task successfully.' (Mandler, 1980). However, Mandler does not think that the generate–recognize model is 'the primary or preferred memory strategy'.

So we can see that the majority of theories are progressing towards an agreement that people have at least two strategies of recall available to them, and the major contenders for these strategies are direct-access retrieval and generate–recognize retrieval. The theories differ chiefly as to whether one of these routes is favoured over the other, or whether the subject has complete flexibility to choose a recall strategy based on either, or both, of them.

3 Executive control

Where working memory fits into all this is that the central executive of the working memory system is thought of as being in control of cognitive strategies. The findings of working memory experiments described in Part II demonstrate that we are able to enhance memory performance by shifting items to short-term stores (e.g. the articulatory loop and the visuo-spatial scratch pad). Holding some items in short-term memory reliably is clearly a very important facility — such a memory is vital for many problem-solving tasks, for example. The executive control system clearly has many strategies available to it to provide flexibility in processing. All the dual-process or dual-route models require an executive to control potentially competing strategies for recall or recognition. For example, the executive must decide when it is no longer worth trying to recall via one route and it is necessary to try another.

The executive has many other functions in memory. For example metamemory ability (knowing what you know or don't know) resides in the executive. While we can model memories as representations of knowledge held in some kind of store, it seems implausible that absent or unknown facts are individually encoded as unknown. So how do we judge that we definitely don't know something? Perhaps the executive, when interrogating memory with cues that it has created or been provided with, is able to evaluate the response of the memory system in such a way that it can infer that there is no relevant representation in memory.

A similar question is how we know that we have really experienced something, as opposed to dreaming or imagining it. The phenomenon of reality monitoring was discussed in Part I. Most people are very good at this: if this discrimination breaks down severely, the symptoms are decidedly schizophrenic. This normally high reliability probably comes from the executive's ability to search for various tell-tale attributes on the memory traces, such as sensory, spatial and temporal codings. But this discrimination can go wrong, and may even be misled, as the research on eye-witness testimony shows, since under certain circumstances new and/or incorrect information can be incorporated into memory traces and may subsequently not be distinguished from reality.

4 Conclusion

Part I started by drawing attention to the many different characteristics of memory which are involved in everyday life, ranging from short-term memory for telephone numbers to long-term memory for childhood events. Memories include general knowledge of facts stored in semantic memory and memory of experiences in episodic memory, including episodes of learning lists of words in the laboratory. So what have we learnt from the many experiments described in Parts II and III?

Memory research has demonstrated that human memory systems comprise a set of encoding and retrieval operations, all governed by a flexible central executive. Psychologists can measure the effects of complex operations involved in encoding and retrieval, although it is not always easy to assign the various processes to a specific stage of information processing. Perhaps the biggest grey area remaining is the central executive, which is crucial to flexible strategies for using memory in real-life tasks. Baddeley and Hitch describe this as the remaining area of ignorance. As more and more research examines human information processing of all kinds, psychologists hope to increase our understanding of what the central executive does and the strategies it can use. Of course, the major feature of the executive system is not only its ability to deploy known strategies for encoding and retrieval, but its unsurpassed ability (on earth at least) to devise and use entirely new strategies to solve new problems as it comes across them. We must never forget that the study of memory looks at just a small fraction of the total cognitive processing system.

Answers to SAQs

SAQ 1
(a) and (b) should be accessible to introspection because they are fairly slow processes with several component steps. (c) is so automatic and (d) so instantaneous that there is little or no conscious insight into the processes involved. (e) may sometimes involve a slow search or processes of trial and error that can be reported, but sometimes the solution just 'pops up' and the solver has no idea what processes produced it.

SAQ 2
Cooker, sink and teapot would have high schema expectancy in a kitchen and would be most likely to be remembered. Hat and stethoscope would have low schema expectancy and would be less likely to be recalled. Items like pots and pans, that are very probable objects in a kitchen, might be falsely recalled if they were not actually present.

SAQ 3
Group A tend to give a higher estimate of the speed. Their judgment is influenced by the word 'smashed', which implies greater impact and higher speed.

SAQ 4
(a) Discrimination failure: confusing the objects involved in the actions.
(b) Subroutine failure: component actions wrongly ordered.
(c) Test failure: switching goals.

SAQ 5
A real event is usually distinguishable from a dream event because you can remember the context and circumstances surrounding it, and a coherent chain of preceding and subsequent events. Dream events are like imagined events in that they usually lack a coherent context of this kind.

SAQ 6
(a) and (c) are semantic knowledge; (b) and (d) are episodic knowledge. (a) and (c) are general factual statements; (b) and (d) contain specific details, and refer to a specific occasion.

SAQ 7
Experimenter A used science fiction stories. The old people had less expert knowledge on this topic and so did worse than the young people. Experimenter B used plots of 1940s films. The old people had expert knowledge of these and did as well or better than the young.

SAQ 8
The answer is (b), because in this condition people can make use of previous knowledge to reduce the memory load. Most people would not have known the trade deficit figures for 1975 so (c) does not help.

SAQ 9
Generally speaking, adults have a greater memory span than children. In part, this reflects greater verbal skills, but more importantly the fact that chunking enhances memory span usually gives adults a greater advantage.

SAQ 10
(a) Primary acoustic store, central executive, possibly articulatory loop.
(b) Articulatory loop, central executive.
(c) Possibly all four components.

SAQ 11
Firstly, the attentional resources of the central executive would be required. Since the problems are presented visually, the visuo-spatial scratch pad might be involved. Finally, the fact that the task involves verbal material where the order of the letters is important suggests the likely use of the articulatory loop.

SAQ 12
While it may often seem obvious whether an orienting task involves deep or shallow processing, there is actually no proper objective method of making the decision. Accordingly, while some doubts may be raised about the decisions made by Hyde and Jenkins, the matter cannot be resolved.

SAQ 13
The reason is that the effects of processing activities on memory are affected to a large extent by a range of other factors such as the nature of the retention test and the learning skills of the individual subject.

SAQ 14

Type of trace structure	Probability of occurrence
AR	70%
A	10%
R	15%
null	5%

It really is that simple!
  Do not be confused by this exact correspondence between the numbers in the summary table of results of the reduction method and the numbers in the table of types of trace structure. Interpreting the numbers as the probability of occurrence of memory trace types is a theoretical step which results from the Encoding Specificity Principle.

SAQ 15
First, the cell for associate cue *success* and rhyme cue *failure*. Because we ignore performance after a cue's *success*, we must use the situation when *failure* occurred first. This means the figure from the table in which the rhyme cue was first, for associate cue success and rhyme cue failure, is used (16%). We enter this figure in Cell 2 of the results table.
  Next, we do the cell for associate cue *failure* and rhyme cue *success*. Now we ignore performance after rhyme cue success when it was the first cue, so we use data from the results when the *associate* cue was first. The figure from this table for associate cue failure and rhyme cue success is 14%, which we enter in Cell 3 of the results table.
  When both cues have failed, we don't have to ignore any data. So we can make

Answers to SAQs

up the last cell from the average of the results in both tables for both cues failing. The two results are 35% and 45%, so the final value is $(35+45) \div 2 = 40\%$, which we enter into Cell 4.

Finally, when both cues succeed, we cannot use any data from the original results, since we have to ignore all data after success on the first cue. However, since we know that all four cells must add up to 100%, we can find Cell 1 by subtracting the sum of the other three cells from 100%.

This gives $100 - (14 + 16 + 40) = 100 - 70 = 30\%$. This figure is put in Cell 1, giving a final table of:

		Rhyme cue	
		Success	Failure
Associate cue	Success	1 30%	2 16%
	Failure	3 14%	4 40%

SAQ 16

I give two answers, the first using fractions expressed as percentages, and the second expressing fractions as decimals. If your calculator doesn't have percentage calculation available, you can look at the second set of working.

For Cell 2:

$$
\begin{aligned}
\text{Cell 2} &= T_r \times (100\% - R_s) \times A_s & &= T_r \times (1 - R_s) \times A_s \\
&= 50\% \times (100\% - 40\%) \times 60\% & &= .5 \times (1 - .4) \times .6 \\
&= 50\% \times 60\% \times 60\% & &= .5 \times .6 \times .6 \\
&= 18\% & &= .18
\end{aligned}
$$

For Cell 3:

$$
\begin{aligned}
\text{Cell 3} &= T_r \times R_s \times (100\% - A_s) & &= T_r \times R_s \times (1 - A_s) \\
&= 50\% \times 40\% \times (100\% - 60\%) & &= .5 \times .4 \times (1 - .6) \\
&= 50\% \times 40\% \times 40\% & &= .5 \times .4 \times .4 \\
&= 8\% & &= .08
\end{aligned}
$$

For Cell 4:

$$
\begin{aligned}
\text{Cell 4} &= T_r \times (100\% - R_s) \times (100\% - A_s) + (100\% - T_r) \\
&= 50\% \times (100\% - 60\%) \times (100\% - 40\%) + (100\% - 50\%) \\
&= 50\% \times 40\% \times 60\% + 50\% \\
&= 12\% + 50\% \\
&= 62\%
\end{aligned}
$$

or in decimals:

$$
\begin{aligned}
\text{Cell 4} &= T_r \times (1 - R_s) \times (1 - A_s) + (1 - T_r) \\
&= .5 \times (1 - .6) \times (1 - .4) + (1 - .5) \\
&= .5 \times .4 \times .6 + .5 \\
&= .12 + .5 \\
&= .62
\end{aligned}
$$

SAQ 17

Such manipulations might be: varying the instructions given to subjects before they read the items to be remembered, using various interfering tasks during the time between presentation of the items and the recall test, or varying the conditions and the context under which the recall test is carried out.

160

SAQ 18

(a) The experiment used a cued recall test and a recognition test.
(b) The recall test used weak associate cues which had been presented along with the target item, while the recognition test used a copy of the target item as a cue.
(c) The aim was to show that there are items which can be recalled but not recognized.
(d) The phenomenon is called 'recognition failure of recallable words' (or just *recognition failure* for short).
(e) The experiment is very similar to the reduction method, since two different recall tests, using two different cues, are used to investigate the structure of the memory trace.

References

AITKENHEAD, A. M. and SLACK, J. M. (1985) *Issues in Cognitive Modeling*, Erlbaum.

ALBA, J. W. and HASHER, L. (1983) 'Is memory schematic?' *Psychological Bulletin*, 93, pp. 203–31.

ALLPORT, D. A. (1980) 'Attention and performance' in G. Claxton (ed.) *Cognitive Psychology: New Directions*, Routledge and Kegan Paul.

ANDERSON, J. R. and REDER, L. (1979) 'An elaborative processing explanation of depth of processing' in L. S. Cermak and F. I. M. Craik (eds) *Levels of Processing in Human Memory*, Erlbaum.

ATKINSON, R. C. and SHIFFRIN, R. M. (1968) 'Human memory: a proposed system and its control processes' in K. W. Spence and J. T. Spence (eds) *The Psychology of Learning and Motivation*, *Vol. 2*, Academic Press.

ATKINSON, R. C. and SHIFFRIN, R. M. (1971) 'The control of short-term memory', *Scientific American*, 225, pp. 82–90.

BADDELEY, A. D. (1968) 'A three-minute reasoning test based on grammatical transformation', *Psychonomic Science*, 10, pp. 341–2.

BADDELEY, A. D. (1979) 'Working memory and reading' in P. A. Kolers, M. E. Wrolstad and H. Bouma (eds) *Processing of Visible Language*, Plenum.

BADDELEY, A. D. (1981a) 'The concept of working memory: a view of its current state and probable future development', *Cognition*, 10, pp. 17–23.

BADDELEY, A. D. (1981b) 'Reading and working memory', *Bulletin of the British Psychological Society*, 35, pp. 414–17.

BADDELEY, A. D., ELDRIDGE, M. and LEWIS, V. J. (1981) 'The role of subvocalisation in reading', *Quarterly Journal of Experimental Psychology*, *33a*, pp. 439–54.

BADDELEY, A. D. and HITCH, G. (1974) 'Working memory' in G. H. Bower (ed.) *The Psychology of Learning and Motivation*, *Vol. 8*, Academic Press.

BADDELEY, A. D. and LEWIS, V. J. (1981) 'Inner active processes in reading: the inner voice, the inner ear, and the inner eye', in A. M. Lesgold and C. A. Perfetti (eds) *Interactive Processes in Reading*, Erlbaum.

BADDELEY, A. D. and LIEBERMAN, K. (1980) 'Spatial working memory' in R. S. Nickerson (ed.) *Attention and Performance*, *Vol. VIII*, Erlbaum.

BADDELEY, A. D., THOMSON, N. and BUCHANAN, M. (1975) 'Word length and the structure of short-term memory' *Journal of Verbal Learning and Verbal Behavior*, 14, pp. 575–89.

BARTLETT, F. C. (1932) *Remembering*, Cambridge University Press.

BEKERIAN, D. A. and BOWERS, J. M. (1983) 'Eye-witness testimony: were we misled? *Journal of Experimental Psychology: Learning, Memory and Cognition*, 9, pp. 139–45.

BRANSFORD, J. D., FRANKS, J. J., MORRIS, C. D. and STEIN, B. S. (1979) 'Some general constraints on learning and memory research' in L. S. Cermak and F. I. M. Craik (eds) *Levels of Processing in Human Memory*, Erlbaum.

BREWER, W. F. and TREYENS, J. C. (1981) 'Role of schemata in memory for places', *Cognitive Psychology*, 13, pp. 207–30.

BROADBENT, D. E., COOPER, P. F., FITZGERALD, P. and PARKES, K. R. (1982) 'The cognitive failures questionnaire (CFQ) and its correlates', *British Journal of Clinical Psychology*, 21, pp. 1–18.

BROWN, R. and KULIK, J. (1982) 'Flashbulb memory', in U. Neisser (ed.), *Memory Observed*, W. H. Freeman.

CHASE, W. G. and SIMON, H. A. (1973) 'Perception in chess', *Cognitive Psychology*, 4, pp. 55–81.

CHI, M. T. H. (1978) 'Knowledge structures and memory development', in R. S. Siegler (ed.) *Children's Thinking: What Develops?*, Erlbaum.

COHEN, G. (1988) *Memory in the Real World*, Erlbaum.

COHEN, G. and FAULKNER, D. (1984) 'Everyday memory in the over-sixties', *New Scientist*, October.

CRAIK, F. I. M. (1973) 'A "levels of analysis" view of memory' in P. Pliner, L. Krames and T. M. Allomay (eds) *Communication and Affect: Language and Thought*, Academic Press.

CRAIK, F. I. M. and LOCKHART, R. S. (1972) 'Levels of processing: a framework for memory research', *Journal of Verbal Learning and Verbal Behavior*, 11, pp. 671–84.

CRAIK, F. I. M. and TULVING, E. (1975) 'Depth of processing and the retention of words in episodic memory', *Journal of Experimental Psychology: General*, 104, pp. 268–94.

EGAN, D. E. and SCHWARTZ, B. J. (1979) 'Chunking in recall of symbolic drawings', *Memory and Cognition*, 7, pp. 149–58.

EYSENCK, M. W. (1979) 'Depth, elaboration, and distinctiveness' in L. S. Cermak and F. I. M. Craik (eds) *Levels of Processing in Human Memory*, Erlbaum.

EYSENCK, M. W. (1984) *A Handbook of Cognitive Psychology*, Erlbaum.

FLAVELL, J. H. (1963) *The Developmental Psychology of Jean Piaget*, Van Nostrand Reinhold.

GLENBERG, A., SMITH, S. M. and GREEN, C. (1977) 'Type I rehearsal: maintenance and more', *Journal of Verbal Learning and Verbal Behavior*, 16, pp. 339–52.

HAMILTON, P., HOCKEY, G. R. J. and REJMAN, M. (1977) 'The place of the concept of activation in human information processing theory: an integrative approach' in S. Dornic (ed.) *Attention and Performance, Vol. VI*, Erlbaum.

HARDYCK, C. D. and PETRINOVICH, L. F. (1970) 'Subvocal speech and comprehension level as a function of the difficulty level of reading material, *Journal of Verbal Learning and Verbal Behavior*, 9, pp. 647–52.

HARRIS, R. J. (1978) 'The effects of jury size and judge's instructions on memory for pragmatic implications from courtroom testimony', *Bulletin of the Psychonomic Society*, 11, pp. 129–32.

HARRIS, R. J. and MONACO, G. E. (1976) 'Psychology of pragmatic implication: information processing between the lines', *Journal of Experimental Psychology: General*, 107, pp. 1–22.

HEBB, D. O. (1961) 'Distinctive features of learning in the higher animal' in J. F. Delafresnaye (ed.) *Brain Mechanisms and Learning*, Blackwell.

HITCH, G. and BADDELEY, A. D. (1976) 'Verbal reasoning and working memory', *Quarterly Journal of Experimental Psychology*, 28, pp. 603–21.

References

HULICKA, I. M. (1982) 'Memory functioning in late adulthood' in F. I. M. Craik and S. Trehub (eds) *Advances in the Study of Communication and Affect, Vol. 8: Aging and Cognitive Processes*, Plenum Press.

HUEY, E. B. (1908) *The Psychology and Pedagogy of Reading*, Macmillan.

HUNT, E. (1980) 'Intelligence as an information-processing concept', *British Journal of Psychology*, 71, pp. 449–77.

HYDE, T. S. and JENKINS, J. J. (1973) 'Recall for words as a function of semantic, graphic and syntactic orienting tasks', *Journal of Verbal Learning and Verbal Behavior*, 12, pp. 471–80.

JACOBY, L. L. and CRAIK, F. I. M. (1979) 'Effects of elaboration of processing at encoding and retrieval: trace distinctiveness and recovery of initial context' in L. S. Cermak and F. I. M. Craik (eds) *Levels of Processing in Human Memory*, Erlbaum.

JAMES, W. (1899) *Talks to Teachers on Psychology, And to Students on Some of Life's Ideals*, Holt.

JOHNSON, M. K. (1985) 'The origin of memories' in P. C. Kendall (ed) *Advances in Cognitive Behavioural Research and Therapy*, Academic Press.

JOHNSON, M. K. and RAYE, C. L. (1981) 'Reality monitoring', *Psychological Review*, 88, pp. 67–85.

JOHNSON, M. K., RAYE, C. L., WANG, A. and TAYLOR, T. (1979) 'Fact and fantasy: The role of accuracy and variability in confusing imaginations with perceptual experiences', *Journal of Experimental Psychology: Human Learning and Memory*, 5, pp. 229–240.

JONES, G. V. (1978) 'Recognition failure and dual mechanisms in recall', *Psychological Review*, 85, pp. 464–9.

KINTSCH, W. (1978) 'More on recognition failure of recallable words: Implications for generation–recognition models?', *Psychological Review*, 85, pp. 470–3.

LACHMAN, J. L., LACHMAN, R. and THRONESBERRY, C. (1981) 'Meta-memory through the adult life span', *Developmental Psychology*, 15, pp. 543–51.

LABERGE, D. (1981) 'Automatic information processing: a review' in J. Long and A. Baddeley (eds), *Attention and Performance, Vol. IX*, Erlbaum.

LE VOI, M. E., AYTON, P. J., JONCKHEERE, A. R., McCLELLAND, A. G. R. and RAWLES, R. E. (1983) 'Unidimensional memory traces: On the analysis of multiple cued recall', *Journal of Verbal Learning and Verbal Behavior*, 22, pp. 560–76.

LE VOI, M. E. and RAWLES, R. E. (1979) 'Backward recognition failure: a case of retrieval success', *Quarterly Journal of Experimental Psychology*, 31, pp. 609–20.

LEVY, B. A. (1978) 'Speech processing during reading' in A. M. Lesgold, J. W. Pellegrino, S. D. Fokkema and R. Glaser (eds) *Cognitive Psychology and Instruction*, Plenum.

LINTON, M. (1982) 'Transformations of memory in everyday life', in U. Neisser, (ed.) *Memory Observed*, W. H. Freeman.

LOFTUS, E. F. (1975) 'Leading questions and the eye-witness report', *Cognitive Psychology*, 7, pp. 560–72.

LOFTUS, E. F. (1979) 'Reactions to blatantly contradictory information', *Memory and Cognition*, 7, pp. 368–74.

LOFTUS, E. F., MILLER, D. G. and BURNS, H. J. (1978) 'Semantic integration of verbal information into a visual memory', *Journal of Experimental Psychology, Human Learning and Memory*, 4, pp. 19–31.

MANDLER, G. (1980) 'Recognizing: The judgement of previous occurrence', *Psychological Review*, 87, pp. 252–71.

MILLER, G. A. (1956) 'The magical number seven plus or minus two', *Psychological Review*, 63, pp. 81–97.

MORRIS, C. D., BRANSFORD, J. D. and FRANKS, J. J. (1977) 'Levels of processing versus transfer appropriate processing', *Journal of Verbal Learning and Verbal Behavior*, 16, pp. 519–33.

NEISSER, U. (1978) 'Memory: what are the important questions?' in M. M. Gruneberg, P. E. Morris and R. N. Sykes (eds) *Practical Aspects of Memory*, Academic Press.

NEISSER, U. (1982) *Memory Observed*, W. H. Freeman.

NORMAN, D. A. and BOBROW, D. G. (1979) 'Descriptions: an intermediate stage in memory retrieval', *Cognitive Psychology*, 11, pp. 107–23.

NORMAN, D. A. (1981) 'Categorization of action slips', *Psychological Review*, 88, pp. 1–15.

OGILVIE, J. C., TULVING, E., PASKOWITZ, S. and JONES, G. V. (1980) 'Three-dimensional memory traces: A model and its application to forgetting', *Journal of Verbal Learning and Verbal Behavior*, 19, pp. 405–15.

PETERSON, L. R. and PETERSON, M. J. (1959) 'Short-term retention of individual items', *Journal of Experimental Psychology*, 58, pp. 193–8.

RABINOWITZ, J. C., MANDLER, G. and BARSALOU, L. W. (1977), 'Recognition failure: another case of retrieval failure', *Journal of Verbal Learning and Verbal Behavior*, 16, pp. 639–63.

RAYNER, K., CARLSON, M. and FRAZIER, L. (1983) 'The interaction of syntax and semantics during sentence processing: eye movements in the analysis of semantically biased sentences', *Journal of Verbal Learning and Verbal Behavior*, 22, pp. 358–74.

REASON, J. T. (1979) 'Actions not as planned: the price of automatization', in G. Underwood and R. Stevens (eds) *Aspects of Consciousness, Vol. 1*, Academic Press.

REISBERG, D., RAPPAPORT, I. and O'SHAUGHNESSY, M. (1984) 'Limits of working memory: the digit digit-span', *Journal of Experimental Psychology: Learning, Memory and Cognition*, 10, pp. 203–21.

RICHARDSON, J. T. E. (1984) 'Developing the theory of working memory', *Memory and Cognition*, 12, pp. 71–83.

RUBIN, D. C. and KOZIN, M. (1984) 'Vivid memories', *Cognition*, 16, pp. 81–5.

RUMELHART, D. E. and NORMAN, D. A. (1983) 'Representation in memory' in R. C. Atkinson, R. J. Herrnstein, G. Lindzey and R. D. Luce (eds) *Handbook of Experimental Psychology*, Wiley and Sons.

SALAME, P. and BADDELEY, A. D. (1982) 'Disruption of short-term memory by unattended speech: Implications for the structure of working memory', *Journal of Verbal Learning and Verbal Behavior*, 21, pp. 150–64.

SCHANK, R. C. (1981) 'Language and memory' in D. A. Norman (ed.) *Perspectives on Cognitive Sciences*, Erlbaum.

References

SHIFFRIN, R. M. and SCHNEIDER, W. (1977) 'Controlled and automatic human information processing, II: Perceptual learning, automatic attending, and a general theory', *Psychological Review*, 84, pp. 127–90.

SIMON, H. A. (1974) 'How big is a chunk?', *Science*, 183, pp. 482–8.

SPILICH, G. J., VESONDER, G. T., CHIESI, H. L. and VOSS, J. F. (1979) 'Text processing of domain-related information for individuals with high and low domain knowledge', *Journal of Verbal Learning and Verbal Behavior*, 18, pp. 275–90.

SUNDERLAND, A., HARRIS, J. E. and BADDELEY, A. D. (1983) 'Do laboratory tests predict everyday memory? A neuropsychological study', *Journal of Verbal Learning and Verbal Behavior*, 22, pp. 341–57.

THOMSON, D. M. and TULVING, E. (1970) 'Associative encoding and retrieval: Weak and strong cues', *Journal of Experimental Psychology*, 86, pp. 255–62.

TULVING, E. (1972) 'Episodic and semantic memory' in E. Tulving and W. Donaldson (eds) *Organization of Memory*, Academic Press.

TULVING, E. and THOMSON, D. M. (1973) 'Encoding specificity and retrieval processes in episodic memory', *Psychological Review*, 80, pp. 353–73.

TULVING, E. and WATKINS, M. J. (1975) 'Structure of memory traces', *Psychological Review*, 82, pp. 261–75.

WANNER, E. and SHINER, S. (1976) 'Measuring transient memory load', *Journal of Verbal Learning and Verbal Behavior*, 15, pp. 159–67.

WATKINS, M. J. and GARDINER, J. M. (1979) 'An appreciation of generate-recognize theory of recall', *Journal of Verbal Learning and Verbal Behavior*, 18, pp. 687–704.

WHITTEN, W. B. and LEONARD, J. M. (1981) 'Directed search through autobiographical memory', *Memory and Cognition*, 9, pp. 566–79.

WILDING, J. and MOHINDRA, N. (1980) 'Effects of subvocal suppression, articulating aloud and noise on sequence', *British Journal of Psychology*, 71, pp. 247–61.

WILLIAMS, M. D. and HOLLAN, J. D. (1982) 'The process of retrieval from very long term memory', *Cognitive Science*, 5, pp. 87–119.

Index of Authors

Index of Authors

Index of Concepts

Index of Concepts